Decentralization in Ethiopia

I0091274

Edited by

Taye Assefa
Tegegne Gebre-Egziabher

fSS

Forum for Social Studies
Addis Ababa

ISBN-10:99944-50-11-5
ISBN-13:978-99944-50-11-4

Forum for Social Studies (FSS)
P.O. Box 25864 code 1000
Addis Ababa, Ethiopia
Email: fss@ethionet.et
Web: www.fssethiopia.org.et

The Forum for Social Studies gratefully acknowledges the financial support of the Royal Norwegian Embassy, which made it possible to produce this publication.

Contents

List of Figures and Tables

Introduction

*Tegegne Gebre-Egziabher**

A Brief Overview of Decentralization in Ethiopia

In the last quarter century, many countries have engaged in the process of decentralization by transferring responsibilities of the state to lower tiers of government. Such transfer of power is believed to bring not only political stability and contribute to democratic governance, but also improve service delivery and attain equity. The 1991 government change in Ethiopia has ushered in a decentralized system of governance. This is a departure from the past political system which did not allow for self-rule and institutional development and harmony between the different ethnic groups. Decentralization in Ethiopia is hoped to bring about harmony and cooperation between different groups and promote local self-rule.

The decentralization drive in Ethiopia has proceeded in two phases. The first wave of decentralization (1991-2001) was centered on creating and empowering National/Regional Governments and hence was termed as mid-level decentralization (Tegegne 1998). During this period, National/Regional State Governments were established with changes in the local and central government system (Yigremew 2001). The National/Regional Governments were entrusted with legislative, executive and judicial powers in respect of all matters within their areas, and with the exception of those that fall under the jurisdiction of the Federal Government (defense, foreign affairs, economic policy, etc.) (Kasshun and Tegegne 2004). In particular, they are empowered, among others, to issue regional constitutions and other laws, plan and execute social and economic development. Fiscal decentralization which elaborated the sharing of revenue between regions and central governments, and introduced transfers and subsidies, was part of the decentralization process. Fiscal decentralization was intended to assist Regional Governments by boosting their capacity for developing their localities through self-initiative. It is also meant to narrow the existing gaps in economic growth and development among regions (Kasshaun and Tegegne 2004). Despite this, fiscal imbalances between regions and heavy dependence of the Regional Governments on the Federal Government's transfer and subsidies have persisted.

* Institute of Regional and Local Development Studies, Addis Ababa University.

While the first wave of decentralization has registered significant achievements in local governance and regional self-rule, it was not capable of bringing genuine self-rule particularly at lower levels of administration where governance and decentralization matter most. Though the Constitution allows for the creation of weredas with their elected councils, the lack of power, resources and authorities has limited them to effectively engage in democratic self-rule. In addition, Zonal and Regional authorities had a controlling, checking and monitoring power over the activities of Wereda Governments.

These circumstances prompted the Central Government to take an initiative to further devolve powers and responsibilities to the weredas in 2001. This was achieved through the District Level Decentralization Program (DLDP) and Urban Management Program (UMP). Unlike the first wave of decentralization, which has a simultaneous country-wide coverage, the second wave was initially limited to the four Regional States, namely, Oromia, Amhara, Tigray and Southern Nations, Nationalities and Peoples' Region. The process entailed enabling legislation for local governments, fiscal reform, institutional restructuring, capacity development, etc. In terms of the institutional restructuring, Zonal Administrations have undergone a process of scaling down and more powers were accorded to weredas. Weredas are also allowed to establish more offices which were manned by redeploying personnel from the regional and zonal level offices. The main instrument of DLDP, however, is the werdea block grant which made resources available to weredas through transfers from regions. Though the transfer may not be adequate to cover all the expenses of the weredas, it has allowed them to exercise planning and budgeting which was earlier accorded to the Zonal and Regional authorities.

The above is a brief glimpse of the decentralization drive of Ethiopia. While decentralization has changed the political climate of the country, it has certainly led to questions regarding its various procedures, ramifications and impact. Along this line, it is not difficult to see that there is a room for improvement in order to maximize the benefits of decentralization. So far decentralization in Ethiopia has attracted some research and study. A lot, however, remains to be done to get deeper into the decentralization process in Ethiopia, particularly in light of recent developments. Further research and investigation will help to fill knowledge gaps and provide policy makers with adequate sufficient and reliable data to improve the decentralization drive in Ethiopia.

This volume brings together scoping studies made by FSS and other studies of decentralization. The purpose of the scoping study is to identify knowledge gaps for further research and generate debate on decentralization in Ethiopia. The scoping study has two parts. The first one is a literature review which attempts to document existing studies on decentralization in Ethiopia and highlights some research gaps. This part is prepared by Tegegne Gebre-Egziabher and Kassahun Berhanu. The second part is a field work that involved a rapid assessment of eight weredas and two kifle ketemas in Addis Ababa. This part is prepared by Meheret Ayenew. The other three studies included in the volume are synopses of masters theses submitted to the Institute of Regional and Local Development Studies of Addis Ababa University.

Highlights of the Papers

Tegegne and Kassahun present a broad canvas of the different issues of decentralization in Ethiopia. The topics reviewed cover the design, impact and implementation of the decentralization program, in addition to other cross-cutting issues such as non-state actors, gender and environment. Tegegne and Kasshaun note that under the political and legal framework it is important to investigate whether the solemn pledges made are feasible in the face of the diversities of sub-national governments. The ethno-linguistic considerations as a cornerstone of decentralization and regional-local self-rule in Ethiopia need a thorough investigation though at present most authors make only nominal observations. Most of the studies done on fiscal decentralization pertain to the situation prior to the recent wereda-level decentralization. The current arrangements of fiscal decentralization that include region-wereda transfers and wereda fiscal decentralization have barely been investigated. The value added of DLDP and wereda decentralization needs to be rigorously exaamined in order to better understand the ramifications of the recent move in decentralization. Decentralization has various impacts: Service delivery, socio-economic development, poverty reduction. Studies related to accountability of service providers to users, representation and participation of users in planning and decision-making processes, and structures for participation and representation are cited as important areas of investigation. The synergies between decentralization and pro-poor policies are not clearly known to date. This presents an important area of investigation since pointing out how synergies could be attained and exploited is necessary to harmonize decentralization with other policies. Similarly, the impact of decentralization on quality of services and infrastructure need to be examined. Tegegne and Kassahun note that decentralization in Ethiopia is one of the instruments in expediting poverty reduction. Though some desk-based studies along this line have been made, a systematic study investigating the poverty-decentralization link is still yet to come. The authors point out that various studies have highlighted implementation problems such as capacity, resource and other constraints. There is, however, a need to articulate the achievements of the decentralization program.

The relation of environment, gender and non-state actors with decentralization is little studied though these cross-cutting issues are influenced by decentralization. To what extent decentralization has improved environmental protection and resource management, how non-state actors are influenced by and influence decentralization, whether decentralization has brought real empowerment to women are all areas awaiting for further and deeper investigation in Ethiopia.

Meherets' paper is a rapid assessment of wereda decentralization in 8 weredas drawn from four regions. In addition, two kifle ketemas in Addis Ababa were part of the sample. The empirical part of the paper highlights great variation in population size among weredas and in fact questions the assumption made by the wereda decentralization program that weredas have a population size ranging between 100,000-120,000. This has implication not only for present budget allocations but for future redivision of weredas as well. The study of the sample weredas also shows differences in terms of available services (education, health, drinking water). Factors underlying such differences need to be known in order to inform policy for equitable provision of the services in future.

The study notes that weredas are administered by the Executive Committees, otherwise known as *Cabinets*. The chairman of the cabinet is the chief administrator. Cabinet members are drawn from wereda councils and are responsible for the day-to-day running of the economic and social aspects of the wereda. The cabinet is answerable to the council and implements decisions and policies passed by the council. The council members are elected and serve as part-time, non-salaried deliberative bodies and meet four times a year to exercise oversight function over Wereda Executive Committees. The situation in Addis Ababa is different as a temporary structure with one year tenure has been put in place for an interim period.

Meheret notes that representation of women among cabinet members is limited, but they have a higher representation among councils. The levels of qualification and training of cabinet members indicated that though there are differences among weredas, most have diploma, certificate or higher qualifications. The level of qualification in the critical areas of public services, local economic development and good governance, however, is far from desirable.

The absence of competitive party politics at the local level, the predominant presence of underpaid and not so well qualified administrative personnel, the discrepancy between the law and the actual practice are some of the observations made. Meheret emphasizes that the dominance of the ruling part in council and cabinet membership reduces the political space for non-state actors to participate in economic and political issues affecting the locality. This has a negative implication for participatory governance and downward accountability of wereda governments. One of the issues raised by the author is the problem of unfunded mandates which leaves weredas to shoulder responsibilities without adequate means of discharging their responsibilities. Therefore, the service demand of the local people cannot be met by the wereda governments. Weredas at best are using their resources to cover salaries and administrative costs instead of capital projects. The current wereda decentralization also suffers from problems of skilled personnel, equipments and facilities. On the policy front, the author emphasizes that, with the exception of the Amhara region, there is a marked absence of detailed legal/regulatory framework specifying inter-governmental relationships, wereda finance, etc. The author also notes the limited decision-making authority, responsibilities and resources devolved to the Kebele levels of administration. This reduces the possibility of empowering kebeles for improved service delivery.

Among the other three studies, Tesfaye's and Kumera's concentrate on service delivery since the introduction of wereda decentralization. Tesfaye examines decentralized education services in Moretena Jirru and Bereh Aleltu weredas of North Shoa. The assessment was made along four variables: institutional and resource capacity, school personnel, community participation and budget. The wereda education office in Moretena and Jirru is reported to have a problem of durable leadership, unattractive working environment though the situation in Bereh Aleltu is better due its proximity to Addis Ababa. The Kebele Education and Training Board (KETB) and the Parent Teacher Association (PTA) are local institutions created for education service. The KETB is, however, found to be less effective compared to the PTA. The school personnel in the study weredas have lower qualifications than what is required. Staff shortages and poor logistics for school supervisors were also noted. In addition, very low remuneration, lack of housing and even lack of proper classrooms render the working situation in Bereh Aleltu unconducive for provision of quality education.

Community engagement in the delivery and management of schooling is crucial, and is emphasized in the strategy. The form of community engagement, however, is limited to material contribution, which is far from the true sense of empowering the community. In terms of budgetary resources, though the education sector is the highest recipient of the wereda budget, most of it goes to salaries and wages. The budget constraint in Moretena Jirru wereda has posed difficulty to achieve the standard per capita budget allotted to students. Schools in both weredas do not have the mandate of allocating and re-allocating budget, with a consequence of delay in providing school supplies and interruption in the learning process.

The author concludes by saying that though school functions such as construction, recruitment, upgrading, budget allocation are devolved to the wereda level, most of the decisions are undertaken by a few individuals, while community associations, and school personnel are simply implementers. This is in direct contradiction to community empowerment, a fundamental principle of decentralization. This, coupled with the shortages of skilled humanpower and logistics, imply that devolution of power does not necessarily lead to improved service delivery.

Kumera examines the performances and constraints of selected public services: education, health, water supply and rural roads in view of wereda decentralization. The study was conducted in Digelu and Tijo Wereda of Oromia region. The overall performance of the different services were noted to have shown improvements after decentralization. The improvements, however, become negligible when the efforts of actors other than the wereda institutions are disregarded. Financial and humanpower constraints and problems of coordination and participation have contributed to the low performance of the wereda. The absence of commonly designed and agreed upon plans poses difficulty for the wereda government to address the service needs of the community. This means that besides providing adequate budget and resources for improving service delivery, it is imperative to improve the efficiency of the public sector in order to create an effective and responsive system of service delivery.

Mohammed's paper is an evaluation of the performance of the wereda decentralization program. The study was held in Amhara National Regional State with the emphasis on Legambo Wereda of the South Wello Zone. The author notes the achievements and constrains of wereda decentralization. The achievements include the effort to make the three branches of government independent of each other, the effort to decentralize power to wereda government structures, the effort to launch a pool system, the application of fiscal decentralization, and the effort to generate resources from the people for local development. The constraints include shortage of well-trained, experienced and committed pool of humanpower and lack of competence among members of the political leadership. These constraints are believed to be related to the lack of proper training and motivation.

References

Kassahun Berhanu and Tegegne Gebre-Egziabher. 2004. Citizen participation in the decentralization process in Ethiopia. A consultancy report submitted to the Ministry of Capacity Building, GoE, Addis Ababa.

Tegegne Gebre-Egziabher. 1998. The influences of decentralization on some aspects of local and regional development planning in Ethiopia. *Eastern Africa Social Science Research Review*, vol. 14, No. 1.

Yigremew Adal. 2001, Decentralization and local governance in post-Dergue Ethiopia. In *Proceedings of the Conference on Governance and Sustainable Development: Promoting Collaborative Partnership*, edited by Berhanu Mengistu *et al*. Addis Ababa.

I

A Literature Review of Decentralization in Ethiopia

Tegegne Gebre-Egziabher and *Kassahun Berhanu**

1. Introduction

This literature review was undertaken as part of a scoping study launched by the Forum for Social Studies in 2006. Its aims are to identify major studies conducted to date on decentralization in Ethiopia, provide an overview of their important findings on the processes and challenges of decentralization and determine the knowledge gap relating to the subject in question with a view to setting research priorities.

The review examines works (consultancy reports, research undertakings, etc.) undertaken by others with the reviewers making their observations on several of the issues raised. It is to be noted, however, that one distinct contribution of this undertaking is the effort made to identify gaps and issues that need to be addressed in further research. This is provided in a separate section titled "The Way Forward".

The general approach of the review is to examine the design of the Ethiopian decentralization scheme within the political context in which the process unfolded and in the light of existing legal frameworks governing modes of operation, underlying goals and objectives that are sought to be achieved, and relationships between the different structures and tiers of government charged with the responsibility of expediting the decentralization process. The processes involved in the reorganization of the Ethiopian state structure following the 1991 regime change, which is characterized by changes in the form of government (from unitary to federal) and governance (from the highly centralized to the decentralized variant) were highlighted so as to provide a clear background to the decentralization process under review.

Fiscal decentralization is an important feature of decentralization assessed in the review. The review noted that resource constraints, among others, posed a major impediment in realizing the objectives of

* Department of Political Science and International Relations, Addis Ababa University

decentralization in several respects. One of the distinct features of fiscal decentralization in Ethiopia is the newly introduced block grants scheme that came on the scene following the recent decentralization initiative. Block grants are intergovernmental transfers of funds from regional to wereda governments according to a predetermined formula and with minimum conditionality. In introducing the block grant scheme, it was hoped that wereda governments would be enabled to implement their administrative and development plans without undue interference from higher tiers of authority thereby creating bringing situations closer to genuine local self-rule.

The recent initiatives of the Government of Ethiopia herald the launching of a second phase of decentralization. This was prompted by the need to overcome shortcomings accruing from limiting decentralization to the regional level as was the case during the period between 1991/92 and 2001/02. The government's realization of the consequences thereof culminated in the coming into being of what came to be known as the District-Level Decentralization Program (DLDP). In addition to the already mentioned block grant scheme, the new move is signified by redeployment of skilled and experienced personnel/functionaries to serve in local government sector offices, wereda autonomy in activity and budgetary planning, expanded freedom of operation in terms of raising and putting to use resources originating from "own" revenue sources, hiring required staff, etc.

The review brought to light a number of shortfalls resulting from inadequacy of resources (humanpower and finance), inexperience and lack of awareness, poor coordination and low level of institutionalization, etc. Another aspect of the second generation of decentralization measures introduced recently pertains to municipal decentralization, which was almost totally neglected for over a decade following the 1991 regime change. This was owing to the overemphasis put on reforms regarding rural development and provincial government to the detriment of required reforms in urban development and administration.

In spite of the fact that it has been only a short time since the recent decentralization scheme came on the scene, the review has attempted to determine the impacts of decentralization from the point of view of the major driving forces and factors that prompted its initiation: service delivery, socio-economic development, poverty reduction, planning and management, participation and empowerment, and improved environmental protection. The review examined the state of affairs during the post-decentralization years in terms of quality and efficient service delivery, performance and accountability of service providers, progress with regard to poverty reduction endeavours, and the situation relating to participation and empowerment of citizens and communities. An attempt was also made to determine whether outcomes during the period in question were related with moves made in the direction of deepening the decentralization drive. The review also made an assessment regarding the implementation of the decentralization program by considering issues associated with capacity and institution building, gender mainstreaming, and the role and place of non-state actors in the overall exercise of decentralization. Some topics in the review have thin literature and therefore it was not possible to provide adequate information. This could be an indication of a gap in research on decentralization in the country.

Finally, it is worth noting that the review was conducted between August and October 2006 covering literature that were accessible at the time of writing. Some literature on the issue of decentralization in Ethiopia might not have been examined owing to lack of easy access. These include, among others, the series of reports related to municipal decentralization and impacts of decentralization on human development, prepared by GTZ and Urban Institute for the Ministry of Works and Urban Development and the World Bank, respectively.

2. Design of the Ethiopian Decentralization Drive

2.1. Political Context and Legal Framework

Following the ouster of the military regime in May 1991, a political process that tried to address the issue of local self-rule was immediately initiated by the EPRDF-led Transitional Government. The point of entry in this regard was the promulgation of the Transitional Period Charter (TGE 1991), which contains pertinent provisions in this regard (see Chapter I, Article two, sub-articles a, b and c). Accordingly:

> The right of nations, nationalities, peoples to self-determination is affirmed. To this end, each nation, nationality and people is guaranteed the right to: a) preserve its identity and have it respected, promote its culture and history, and use and develop its language; b) administer its own affairs within its own defined territory and effectively participate in the central government on the basis of freedom and fair and proper representation; c) exercise its right to self-determination of independence, when the concerned nation/nationality and people is convinced that the above rights are denied, abridged or abrogated (TGE 1991).

The Charter outlined a framework for decentralized self-rule in a manner that could be viewed as a major departure at least at the level of official policy. Self-governing units, which meet laid down criteria to qualify as such, were thus entitled to participate in the central government. At the same time they were empowered to run administrative and other undertakings in areas under their respective jurisdiction. A federal arrangement stipulating the need for sharing of powers and functions as an expression of regional and local self-rule was deemed essential owing to its benefits in terms of enhancing socio-economic development, establishing peace and stability, and forging national unity and cohesion on the basis of voluntary coexistence and equality. The policy was justified as the only way out to avert possibilities of disintegration that seemed imminent on the eve of the 1991 regime change. In order to lend legal force to this drive, the Transitional Government of Ethiopia (TGE) enacted a proclamation providing for the establishment of national/regional self-governments in 1992.

The various chapters and articles of Proclamation No. 7/1992 (TGE 1992) dwell on a wide variety of issues ranging from rationales and justifications on the need for such a project to tiers and hierarchy, jurisdiction and competence, structures and powers, accountability and power sharing arrangements concerning sub-national governments at various levels. As opposed to former policy settings and practices, the Proclamation clearly stipulated that all leading bodies at the various levels of local administration would assume a purely representative nature where the incumbency of leading officials of state governments can be realized through periodic elections to be exercised by the eligible electorate in all constituencies.

2.1.1. Devolution and Sub-National Governance and Accountability

Accordingly, 14 national regional state governments were initially constituted on the basis of ethno-linguistic criteria of qualification. Whereas two regions, namely, the cities of Dire Dawa and Addis Ababa were accorded administrative status on the basis of special considerations, five regions collectively established a larger regional entity, namely, the Southern Nationalities, Nations, and Peoples' National/Regional State (SNNPRS) thereby bringing the number of federating regions to nine: Tigray, Afar, Amhara, Oromia, Benishangul-Gumuz, Gambella, SNPPRS, Somali, and Harari. The new arrangement abolished the "awraja" (sub-province) tier by making the "wereda" (district) the lowest unit of local government. In both the urban and rural areas "kebele" administrations (KAs) became grassroots units of government.

The Constitution of the Federal Democratic Republic of Ethiopia (FDRE 1995) forms the legal basis for ensuring citizen voice and participation in socio-economic and political processes. Legal and institutional arrangements aimed at ensuring interface between the government and citizens of Ethiopia are enshrined in the pertinent provisions of the constitution. In particular, Article 43 (sub-article 2) categorically spells out that citizens have the right to "participate in national development and, in particular, to be

consulted with respect to policies and projects affecting their community".
Article 8 of the constitution affirmed that sovereignty resides in the peoples of
Ethiopia who exercise sovereign power through their elected representatives.
Representatives assume offices in leading bodies of government on the basis
of the mandate they obtain as a result of participation of citizens in periodic
elections that take place in accordance with established schedule and rules and
regulations.

The significance of the decentralization drive to local and grassroots
empowerment lies in the fact that different levels of sub-national units of
government are constituted on the basis of citizen participation in the political
process by way of exercising electoral rights. If strictly applied, pertinent
constitutional provisions render citizen voice crucial for the formation and
operation of government structures thereby signifying the importance of the
popular will in influencing decisions of major significance. Citizens are also
legally empowered to recall their elected representatives provided the latter are
found to be at fault as regards their behaviors and actions that run contrary to
their responsibilities and mandates.

It is to be recalled that constitutional provisions that empower citizens
by providing opportunities for access to services, the right of censuring the
behaviors and actions of state institutions and functionaries, participating in
decision making processes with regard to planning, resource and expenditure
management, etc., are complemented by other sets of policies. These include
the Sustainable Development and Poverty Reduction Program (SDPRP), the
Civil Service Reform and Capacity Building Programs, and Wereda
Decentralization, among others.

The Federal and Regional Constitutions define the powers and
functions of regional and local governments in Ethiopia. These include both
political and economic areas of jurisdiction and competence. The former are
expressed in terms of maintaining and enforcing law and order, enacting
constitutions and other legislations, and organizing police forces. The
economic functions range from administering resources to developing and
executing development policies and plans. According to Article 50 (4) of the
federal constitution, regional states can establish their own government and
create other administrative levels that are found to be necessary and
appropriate. These lower units of government are supposed to be provided
with adequate power in a manner that could enable the people to participate
directly in the exercise of self-rule.

The administrative and governance structures of regions and weredas
are organized in a manner that resembles organization of the machinery of the
state at the federal level. Councils posing as legislative bodies are established
on the basis of periodic election outcomes whereby those who got the majority
of votes in their respective constituencies qualify as council members. These
are unicameral legislatures known as state and wereda councils instituted at

regional and local levels, respectively. The executive bodies, alias cabinets, of regional and wereda governments originate from their respective councils on the basis of elections by council members. The councils elect their chairpersons who automatically qualify as chief administrators of regions and weredas. These, in turn, select candidates to fill cabinet posts subject to the approval of their respective legislative bodies. The third branch of government at regional and wereda levels, namely, the judiciary, is instituted as follows: The heads of regional governments nominate the presidents and vice presidents of the regional supreme courts who assume their positions following approval of their appointments by the regional councils. Other regional judicial posts are filled by persons who are nominated by the regional judicial administration commissions whose appointment is subject to endorsement by the regional councils. At this juncture, it is worthy to note that where fusion of powers in Ethiopia is demonstrated at the federal level, sub-national entities in the country are made to follow suit.

Regions have established zones as intermediate tiers of government (liaising between regions and weredas) in their respective areas and facilitate administrative and developmental functions by way of technical assistance. The third tier of government is the wereda (district) administration, which is defined constitutionally and possesses the three arms of government: the council, the executive and the judiciary. Each regional state defines the powers and functions of zonal and wereda administrations in its constitution. Below the wereda is the kebele administration, which has similar functions with weredas though at a lower level.

2.1.2. Relations between Different Tiers of Sub-National Government

Relations between regional, zonal, wereda and kebele administrations that form sub-national levels of government in descending order of hierarchy are characterized by a host of features and underpinned by dual accountability to their respective constituencies, on one hand, and the respective upper tiers on the other (Kassahun and Tegegne 2004). Accordingly, regional governments are constitutionally empowered to establish different levels of state administrations under their respective jurisdictions, enact and execute state constitutions and other laws, formulate and execute economic, social and development policies, strategies/plans, administer land and other natural resources, levy and collect taxes falling under their revenue sources, establish and administer state police forces, etc., without prejudice to the competence, powers and prerogatives of the federal government.

With the exception of those in SNNPRS, zonal administrations are appointed by regional governments to serve as intermediate tiers liaising between regional and local governments while at the same time providing technical and administrative assistance to the latter. In SNNPRS, however, while the role and functions of zones essentially remains the same as in the other regions, the mode and manner of their formation and the legal basis of their existence vary. This is signified by the fact that leading positions in SNNPRS zones are filled through periodic elections of zonal councils and cabinets. Hence their existence and competence is sanctioned by state constitutions thereby lending them legitimacy based on the mandate of the electorate. Notwithstanding the mode and manner of their coming into being, however, all zones in the federating regions of the Ethiopian political system are accountable to their respective regional governments. In SNNPRS, zones are dually accountable to the regional state and the electorate in the weredas. Zones are charged with the responsibility of coordinating the activities of weredas, ensuring preservation and protection of cultural heritages and maintaining law and order in their areas, and monitoring implementation of policies and laws enacted by the regional governments.

Wereda administrations implement policies, laws, plans, directives, and guidelines of regional governments and coordinate activities of wereda executive organs/sector offices. They are also responsible for overseeing socio-economic and developmental activities in kebeles under their jurisdiction. Previously the practice was that wereda administrations depended on zonal units with regard to technical support and administrative facilitation. In effect, weredas were accountable to zones in spite of the fact that the latter were created to facilitate rapport between local and regional governments. Following the 2001/02 wereda decentralization drive, weredas are empowered to enjoy planning, fiscal, and administrative autonomy. They also retained their jurisdiction over kebele administrations.

On the basis of indicative guidelines provided by wereda governments, kebele administrations prepare plans in consultation with sub-kebeles and government teams, the results of which are kebele consolidated plans. Budgeted activities to be undertaken in a given fiscal year are subsequently identified by specifying the amount to be covered through government allocations and community contributions (finance, labor, material). This is followed by approval of the plans by kebele cabinets, which seek formal endorsement from the councils. The wereda cabinets and councils finally decide on these by considering availability of budget and without overlooking the primacy of national and regional priorities. What is important to note here is that citizens make their preferences and voices known regardless of whether these are given due consideration or not. A recent study (Dom and Mohammed 2006, 6) affirmed the existence of some form of sectoral bottom-up planning where there is some kind of needs assessment undertaken at the community level through Development Agents (DAs) by identifying priorities with model farmers, development team leaders, and health workers. Though this approach could be commended for avoiding top-down approaches by inducing the indirect participation of the community through selected actors, direct participation of citizens in the exercise has not been realized to date.

2.2. Fiscal Decentralization

The Ethiopian decentralization has devolved resources and finance to lower levels of government. Proclamation no. 33/1992 is the most important legal instrument in the fiscal decentralization of Ethiopia. The proclamation defined the sharing of revenue between the central government and national/regional governments. The proclamation, among others, specified the basis for revenue sharing, expenditure and revenue assignment, subsidy (grants) and borrowing (TGE 1992).

2.2.1. Expenditure Assignment

Scholars acknowledge that there is no universally acceptable formula in allocating functions between various levels of government, but each country has to tackle the issue based on its own individual circumstances (Eshetu 1994). Notwithstanding this fact, however, some consensus exists regarding the proper jurisdiction of certain functions. Defense, foreign affairs, international and inter-regional trade, currency, highway construction, immigration, civil aviation, environmental legislation are usually the common territories of the central government while police, local roads, utilities, water sewerage, street lighting, cleaning are considered as the responsibilities of regional governments (Eshetu 1994; Girma 1994). In the Ethiopian case Proclamation no. 7/92, which provides for the establishment of national-self government, Proclamation no. 41/92, which provides for the functions of Ministers and Bureaus, together define the functions assigned to regions (see Annex 1). Some scholars observe that the assignment is ambiguous due to its condensed form (Eshetu 1994). Expenditure assignment follows functional assignment and it is worth examining how expenditure distribution between different levels of governments fares.

Eshetu (1994) studied the distribution of expenditure between the central government and the regions based on the 1993/94 budget. It was found out that the share of regions in terms of recurrent expenditure was only slightly over 37% while the bulk of the expenditure was allocated to the central government. In some sectors, however, regions had pronounced shares. The sectors which had the highest share were the social sectors (77.6%), economic services (58.3%), public order (65.8%) while the sectors with the lowest shares were defense (25.5%), and other expenditures (8.85) including external debt service payments. The pattern of the regions' shares in the capital budget was found out to be similar to that of recurrent expenditure. Regions had the highest share in the social sectors such as education (73.7%) and health (87.8%) while regional share in the economic sectors was relatively low (28.3%) (Eshetu 1994). The latter was due to the fact that most of the expenditure in trade, transport, industry, mining, energy was borne by the center while regions concentrated on agriculture and natural resources (Eshetu 1994).

Getachew (2001) presented data on the distribution of recurrent and capital expenditure between the regions and the center for the years 1993/94 through 1997/98. The major observations made by the author concerning recurrent expenditure were: 1) the share of regions in total recurrent expenditure increased from 38% in 1993/94 to 43 % in 1996/97 though the center still accounted for the bulk of the expenditure; 2) Regions' share in social services increased from 75% in 1993/94 to 81% in 1996/97; 3) Regions' share in economic services increased from 58.9% in 1993/94 to 75% in 1997/98; 4) Regions' share in general services increased from 26.8% in 1993/94 to 33% in 1996/97. The author noted that by 1999/00 most of the increase in the regional share of recurrent expenditure saw a decline (Getachew 2001). For instance Regions' share in social services and economic services dropped to 70% and 65%, respectively, in the year 1999/00. The decline could be due to the Ethio-Eritrea war. The trend in regions' share of capital expenditure followed the patterns of recurrent expenditure. For instance, regions' total capital expenditures increased from 33 % in 1993/94 to 62% in 1997/98 with regions' share of social development growing from 63.6% in 1993/94 to 80% in 1997/98 and economic development growing from 23 % in 1993/94 to 53% in 1997/98.

The major observation from the above is that regions are increasing their share of expenditure in both recurrent and capital budget though capital budgets seem to be less decentralized than recurrent expenditure. In terms of sectors, social services are more decentralized than economic services in both recurrent and capital budgets.

2.2.2. Revenue Assignment

Proclamation no. 33/1992 defines revenue assignment dealing with both tax base sharing and revenue sharing. The major objectives of the revenue assignment are to: 1) enable the Central Government and the National/Regional Governments to carry out their duties and responsibilities, 2) help the national/regional governments develop their region on their own initiative, 3) narrow the gap in development and economic growth between regions, 4) encourage activities that are of common interests to regions (TGE 1992). The proclamation also states the criteria of assigning revenue sources such as ownership of source of revenue, the national or regional character of the sources of revenue, levying and collection convenience of tax or duty, population, distribution of wealth, and level of development of each region and factors that enhance integrated and balanced economy (TGE 1992).

Revenue sources in Ethiopia are assigned as central, regional and joint (see annex 2). Eshetu (1994) raises a number of issues regarding the allocation of revenues. These include: 1) the extent of regions' power to levy dues and taxes since Proclamation no. 33/1992 qualifies the regions' power considerably. The proclamation states that the rates of taxes reserved for joint use by the centre and the region are to be determined by the Central Government. The proclamation also states that the tax system shall have a unified policy base with a final word resting in the Ministry of Finance, thus indicating that regions may not have power to determine tax rates even from sources exclusively left for them; 2) implementation problems related to some specific provision that assign some tax sources to regions. In particular the provision that allows regions to appropriate profit tax, personal income tax and sales tax from enterprises owned by regions and taxes collected from rent of houses and properties owned by regions raises a question of equity and efficiency since there are differences in asset base and there is uneven distribution of public enterprises among regions (Eshetu 1994, Getachew 2001); 3) the modality to determine the division of joint revenue between the federal government and regions. The current arrangement is to divide direct taxes in the proportion of 50:50 and domestic indirect taxes in the proportion of 70:30 (Getachew 2001). A study made in 1998, however, observes that joint revenue sources have not benefited regional governments since they are under the management and control of the Central Government (Fenta 1998). In fact at that time some regions indicated that they have no information about joint revenue let alone collect and administer the resource; 4) the adequacy of the revenue sources reserved for the regions particularly in relation to the responsibility entrusted to them. In this regard Befekadu (1994) observes that the fiscal base assigned to the regional governments is very weak and generates revenues far below the level required to fulfill the objectives of fiscal independence; and 5) the allocation of external assistance and grants is not specified in the legislation.

Eshetu (1994) examined the distribution of revenue shares between the Central Government and regions for the 1993/94 budget year. It was found out that the regional share of the total revenue was about 10%. The most important sources of revenue for regions were agricultural income tax, land use fee, rental income tax, stamp sales and duty, charges and fees and the pension contribution. These sources account in the range of 56%-100%. These revenue sources, however, account only for 9.6% of total domestic revenue (Eshetu 1994). On the other hand the share of regions in the most important sources is very low. For example, the share of regions in foreign trade taxes, which account for 32.1% of total revenue, is nil and their share in indirect taxes which account for 22.7% of total revenue is only 11.9% (Eshetu 1994). The trend between 1993/94 through 1997/98 in revenue distribution was examined and the main observations were that regions' share in revenue has increased from 10 % in 1993/94 to 19.7% in 1997/98 (Getachew 2001). The main source of regions' revenue which was important in 1993/94 remains the same during the period 1993/94-1997/98. During these years, a decline in direct taxes and an increase in indirect taxes were noted. The decline in direct taxes could be due to the lowering of income and profit tax rates following the reform program to encourage the private sector participation. A comparison of regions' own revenue with that of regions' total expenditure showed some improvement in the period 1993/94 - 1997/98. In 1993/94 regions were capable of financing 30% of their total expenditure and 41% of their recurrent expenditure from own revenue. The corresponding figures for 1997/98 were 36% and 57% for total expenditure and recurrent expenditure, respectively (Getachew 2001). Though there is an improvement in regions' capacity to finance their own development and running costs, the figures show that regions are not capable of financing both their capital and running costs. The conclusion made by observers is that regional governments have weak revenue sources that are concentrated on direct taxes including personal income tax, which has no historical evidence of sustained growth (Brosio and Gupta cited in Fenta 1998). This instance indicates the incidence of fiscal imbalance in the fiscal decentralization of the country.

2.2.3. *Fiscal Imbalance, Inter-Governmental Transfers and Borrowing*

Fiscal imbalance refers to both vertical and horizontal (regional) imbalances. The former refers to imbalance between revenue means and expenditure needs at different levels of government while the latter refers to regional variations in correspondence between revenue base and expenditure requirements (Kibre 1994).

One of the issues that characterize the fiscal decentralization of Ethiopia is the vertical imbalance. Eshetu (1994) analyzed vertical imbalance in the early 1990s (in particular with reference to the 1993/94 budget) and found out that regions whose share in both recurrent and capital expenditure is about 37%, account for less than 10% of total revenue. The revenue share rises to 20% if foreign assistance and loans are excluded, which is still lower than the expenditure share. It was also mentioned that the rough overall correlation coefficient of vertical imbalance for the 1993/94 budget year was 0.74 (Eshetu 1994). This clearly indicates a striking degree of vertical imbalance in the Ethiopian budget. During this period regions were found to cover only 26% of total expenditure from own revenue and less than half (47.1%) of recurrent expenditure. One possible explanation is the low yielding revenue sources such as agricultural income tax, land use fee, tax on rental income, stamp sales, etc., are assigned to regions while more lucrative sources such as foreign trade taxes, indirect taxes are assigned to the central government. The other explanation is that regions have limited administrative and technical capacity to collect and raise revenue (Fenta 1998). The vertical imbalance trend for the years 1993/94 to 1997/98 showed that the overall correlation coefficient remained at 0.71 for the years 1993/94, 1994/95, and 1995/96 while the coefficients for 1996/97 and 1997/98 were 0.64 and 0.60, respectively (Getachew 2001). Though the trend shows a slight decline, the vertical imbalance in Ethiopia still remains. The vertical imbalance for different regions was also found to be high except for Addis Ababa, which is a region capable of financing its spending from its revenue sources (Getachew 2001). High vertical imbalance by regions indicates their lack of capacity to internalize public expenditure or their dependence on transfers from other parts of the country which has negative implications for their autonomy (Getachew 2001).

Regional (horizontal) imbalance in Ethiopia was also found to have increased between the years 1993/94 through 1997/98. Regional fiscal imbalance (RFI) rose from 31% in 1993/94 to 36% in 1997/98 (Getachew 2001). The large and relatively developed regions (Oromia, Amhara, SNNPR and Tgray) showed an increase in RFI while some emerging regions (Gambella, Benishangul-Gumuz) showed a decline, and other regions such as Afar and Somalia showed fluctuations (Getachew 2001). The increase could be associated with ability to finance spending from own sources of revenue while the decline is a reflection of weak economic base.

The two main types of instruments to deal with vertical imbalance are transfers and borrowing. Both are indicated in Proclamation no. 33/1992. In fact the proclamation states that the purpose of transfers (subsidy) are: "to promote social services and economic development of the national/regional governments, to accelerate the development of the neglected and forgotten areas, to narrow down the gap in per capita income between regions, to support projects that help control negative externalities, to encourage foreign currency earning projects and other projects of national interest" (TGE 1992). The proclamation further states the procedures for obtaining grants from the Central Government. Regions are expected to submit to the Ministry of Finance and the Ministry of Planning and Economic Development, their subsidy requests and their total expenditure requirement. The two ministries review the request in accordance with the objectives set for allocating subsidy (TGE 1992). The proclamation does not indicate the criteria to be used and who decides on the final allocation of the subsidy. As a result during the years 1992/93 and 1993/94, subsidy was allotted on an ad hoc basis depending on the subjective judgments of the evaluating ministries and there was no system to appeal against rejected grant requests.

Since 1994/95, however, budget subsidy has been allocated on the basis of formula that evolved through time. The first introduced in 1994/95 had two separate grant formula, one for capital expenditure and one for recurrent expenditure. For the capital budget, the formula used five variables: population (30%), I-distance (20%), regional tax raising effort (20%), capital expenditure in 1992/93 FY (15%) and the area size of the region (10%) (Gebrehiwet 2002).

Recurrent expenditure was determined on the basis of a number of zones and weredas, structure of bureaus, number of civil servants, length of rural roads to be maintained, previous year budget, number of agricultural demonstration centres (Gebrehiwet 2002). The formula was used since 1995/96 to determine a consolidated budget covering both recurrent and capital expenditures. In addition, the number and weight of variables have changed through time. In 1995/96 the variables used were population, I-distance factor and state revenue to budget ratio with equal weights of 33.3% each. In 1996/97, the 1995/96 variables and weights remained the same except some modifications to the I-distance factor[1]. During the periods 1997/98 through 2000, the three variables used were population (60%), development index (25%), and revenue ratio to budget (15%). The formula during the period 2000/01-2002/03 is composed of four variables: population (55%), development index (25%), revenue raising effort (15%) and poverty level index (10%) (MeDAC cited in Gebrehiwet 2002).

Budget subsidy is the main source of finance for regional governments and the composition of budgets seems to be dominated by treasury. For the SNNP region the treasury accounted for 66 % for the year 2002/03 and 73% for the years 2003/04-2004/05 (Table 1). In Oromia, the treasury accounted for 58 %, 69 % and 67 % for the years 2002/03, 2003/04 and 2004/05, respectively. In contrast, the maximum contribution of regional revenue in both regions is about 20% during the period 2002/03-2004/05 (Table 1).

A study conducted prior to the introduction of DLDP (Tesfaye 2000: 49) affirmed that Oromia and SNNPR receive more than 70% of their total annual revenue on the average in the form of subsidy from the federal government. This implies that there is heavy dependence on the latter denoting that their autonomy is constrained in terms of planning and decision making on the one hand, and the existence of significant influence of the center in directing matters to its liking. Given that Oromia and SNNPR are believed to be relatively better-off than the

---

[1] The I-distance is now determined using six variables instead of the previous eight factors.

"emerging"/peripheral regions (Somali, Afar, Gambella, and Benishangul-Gumuz) in terms of resource base and endowment, the degree and extent of loss of autonomy accruing from increased dependence on the center on the part of the latter is undoubtedly greater.

Table 1. SNNP and Oromia regional budgets by sources (000 birr)

Source	2002/03	%	2003/04	%	2004/05	%
SNNPR						
Treasury	818,600	66	1,001,960	73	1,102,550	73
Loan	129,700	10	92,070	7	41,290	3
Assistance	103,200	8	44,890	4	40,920	3
Regional revenue	187,578.8	16	216,296	16	314,734.1	21
Total	**1,239,098.8**	**100**	**1,366,241**	**100**	**1,510,534.1**	**100**
Oromia						
Treasury	1,274,100	58	1,659,490	69	1,781,840	67
Regional revenue	374,500	17	485,000	20	506,182	19
Loan	218,633	10	97,606	4	81,800	3
Assistance	160,000	7	96,090	4	126,550	4
Retained earnings	177,900	8	82,127	3	177,982	7
Total	**2,205,133**	**100**	**2,420,313**	**100**	**2,674,354**	**100**

SOURCE: Lissane and Mohammed (2005).

Three outstanding issues concerning the grant system in Ethiopia were mentioned by Getachew (2001):

i) Lack of true incentive for revenue generating effort by regional governments;
ii) Budget offset issue;
iii) Dependence on grants.

The first issue relates to periods prior to 2000/01 and it involves reducing subsidy by an amount equal to own revenue of a region and thereby creating disincentive to generate more revenue on the part of regions. This issue, however, has been resolved by suspending the provision since 2000/01 and incorporating a weight of 15% for revenue effort. The second issue still lingers on and it involves reducing the federal budget by the amount of external assistance received by regions. Budget offset system is introduced to meet two objectives: 1) to address regional disparities through promoting equitable distribution of resources among regions, and 2) to protect donors' influence in identifying and formulating national priorities (World Bank citied in Gebrehiwet 2002). Despite these the offset seems to have a major drawback on those regions which are capable of attracting foreign assistance through own effort. The third issue involves arguments to phase out the grant system by resorting to conditional grants and revenue sharing arrangements. The issue of phasing out the grant system should carefully be thought out as it may interfere with the constitutional rights of regions. This implies revising the tax sources of regional and central governments, providing more authority to levy taxes and dues and to determine tax rates. Regions should be encouraged to cover most of their expenditure needs and evolve towards self-sufficiency. This requires a gradual empowerment of regions in raising own resources. The issue of backward or lagging regions should, however, be dealt with by the Central Government in the process of pushing regions to stand on their own.

The other instrument for dealing with fiscal imbalance is borrowing. Proclamation no. 33/1992 states that in order to borrow, regions should submit to the Ministry of Finance and Economic Development, the loan amount and a statement showing the relations of the requested amount with their revenue collection forecast and with economic indicators. The application form should be submitted together with consolidated budget and the feasibility study report of the project for which the loan is required. The Ministry will evaluate the request in light of the national budget deficit and decide what amount regions should borrow and recommend the same to the National Bank of Ethiopia (TGE 1992).

Recently, regions have exercised their rights to borrow by engaging in a loan guarantee system using their own budgets as collateral for fertilizer credit to their farmers. This was found out to have a negative impact on some regions exposed to crop failures and natural disaster which resulted in widespread default by farmers (Getachew 2001).

In general scholars have observed that the privilege of borrowing is very conditional, stringent and problematic (Befekadu 1994). It is conditional in that borrowing is allowed for specific projects and it depends on the debt servicing capacity of regions. The proclamation does not specify who the borrowers are and the sources of credit (Befekadu 1994). The debt servicing capacity of regions vary and particularly regions such as Afar, Benishangul, and Gambella with low capacity can borrow only small amount and this exacerbates the inequality already entrenched in the country (Fenta 1998). In addition given the low revenue capacity of regions, it will not be easy for regions to borrow from banks and financial institutions and the legislation also fails to specify the instrument of borrowing available for regions (Befekadu 1994).

2.2.4. Regional Studies on Fiscal Decentralization

Studies on fiscal decentralization have been conducted in some regions of Ethiopia. Gebrehiwet (2002) looked at expenditure and revenue assignment and the budget subsidy in Tigray region. Both expenditure and revenue assignment during the periods 1993/94-2000/1 were dominated by regional level, with very little role of the local government. In terms of expenditure, it was found out that public expenditure in the region grew from birr 237 million in 1993/94 to birr 366 million in 2000/01, the recurrent/capital ratio grew from 1:1 to a ratio of 1.6:1, the sectoral allocation of expenditure during the period on average showed that the highest was for the social sector (46%) followed by economic sector (33%) and administrative and general service (17%). The average revenue collection during the period was found out to be 71,808,307 birr with an average annual growth rate of 10.3%. Direct tax (45%), indirect tax (31%) and non-tax revenue (24%) contributed to the region's revenue during the time. During this period the region was able to cover only 29.7% of its total expenditure or only 40% of its recurrent expenditure. This is an indication of the region's heavy dependence on the federal government for meeting its expenditure requirement.

In terms of budget subsidy, there is a general trend of increment in the region which according to the author could be attributed to increase in the divisible grant pool and also due to the changes in the allocation formula. For the period 1993/94-2000/1, external sources in Tigray accounted for 22% of the total federal grant. External funds are expected to promote knowledge transfer through introducing new efficient management system and cost effective procurement system and bring in technical expertise (World Bank cited in Gebrehiwet 2002). Despite this the author has found out that officials in the region point out the adverse effects of external fund due to its overcrowding effect of federal grant, its high overhead costs and the complex reporting procedure associated with donors that results in the delay of fund release, etc.

Regarding sub-regions, zones in Tigray region covered only 38% of their recurrent expenditure during the period 1999-2001. The shares of direct tax, indirect tax and non-tax revenue at zonal levels were 56%, 24% and 20%, respectively. Social, administration and general service and economic sectors with shares of 43%, 40% and 17%, respectively, were the major expenditure categories at zonal level. The weredas in Tigray show a high horizontal fiscal imbalance with lowland weredas being the weakest in their fiscal capacity compared to highland weredas.

Melkamu (2004) studied fiscal decentralization in Benishangul-Gumuz by examining trends between 1996/7-2002/03 in expenditure assignment, revenue decentralization, fiscal subsidy and federal subsidy. In

Benishangul the regional sector offices spend 100% of the capital expenditure while weredas participate in some recurrent expenditure spending (59%); the share of local governments in total expenditure is only 31% as opposed to 69% of the region's sectoral offices; the trend in capital and recurrent budget in the region shows a declining trend for the former while the latter seems to show an increase in the years 1996/7 through 2003/04; sectoral allocation within the region shows that economic development particularly construction has shown a dramatic increase from 2.1 % in 1996/97 to 60.4 % in 2002/03. Social development has also shown an increase between 1996/7 (23%) to 32.5% in 2002/03 while general development has shown a decline from 75% in 1996/7 to 7.1 % in 2002/03. The major source of revenue in the region is the federal subsidy (93%).

2.3. Local Level (wereda) Decentralization

Measures of decentralization-cum-devolution introduced in the immediate aftermath of the May 1991 regime change brought about a situation whereby two-levels of government, federal and regional, became operational (Tegegne and Kassahun 2004). For nearly a decade (1992-2001/2002), the decentralization-cum-devolution initiative was limited to the self-governing regions in the sense of exercising devolved powers and functions as stipulated in the pertinent provisions of the federal constitution and other laws. This was expressed by the establishment of elected bodies of governance such as regional unicameral legislatures (councils), executive organs (cabinets), and judicial units in a manner that resembles the structure and organization at the federal level. Regional state governments are also empowered to promulgate their own constitutions without violating the provisions of the federal constitution. Similar branches of government were also instituted at lower levels such as weredas and kebeles, with specified powers and functions. As mentioned earlier, zones are instituted to coordinate administrative activities, prepare development and budget plans, and extend technical assistance to the weredas under them. Except in the Southern Regional State where leading positions at zonal levels are elected, the role of the zones in the remaining constituent regions is more of administrative and technical facilitation without having any constitutional basis. Notwithstanding this, however, zonal administrations exercised a wide range of regulatory powers over weredas, all of which are recognized by the constitution as basic units of local government.

A system of dual accountability underpins the operation of regional and wereda councils whereby each is accountable to its respective constituency and the councils in the next upper tier. Regional councils are answerable to the electorate and the Federal House of Representatives, and enjoy a wide range of powers without prejudice to the competence and prerogatives of the federal government (Tegegne and Kassahun 2004).

Regions are heavily dependent on the federal government in the sense of receiving considerable subsidies through intergovernmental transfers. These are used to overcome budgetary deficits faced by the former. Hence the federal government commands significant leverage in terms of influencing matters to its liking, which also is reflected in region-wereda relations for the same reason. It could thus be argued that the first wave of the decentralization-cum-devolution drive of the period between 1991 and 2001/2002 was mainly limited to the regional level.

The desire for deepening the already initiated decentralization drive of the post-1991 years was reiterated in the poverty reduction program document of the Ethiopian Government, known as *Sustainable Development and Poverty Reduction Program* (SDPRP). The SDPRP underlined that further measures in this regard are crucial "for tackling poverty directly at the grassroots level" (MOFED 2002). The SDPRP also emphasized that there is a need to empower local communities and their institutions in a manner that enables them to participate in processes that affect local livelihoods and wellbeing. It was also claimed that the SDPRP aimed at ensuring that communities in general, and the poor in particular, "are empowered to take full advantage of the opportunities that democratization provides, *inter alia,* through participating in, negotiating with, influencing, controlling, and holding to account the institutions and representatives of wereda and municipal governments (World Bank cited in CIDA 2005).

The Ethiopian decentralization drive of the post-1991 years has taken another step in the devolution of powers and functions to local units of government. Since 2001, practical steps were taken towards empowerment of wereda governments in the four major regions, namely, Tigray, Amhara, Oromia, and SNNPRS. These steps were characterized by new developments such as block grant intergovernmental transfers, power to use own revenue and to generate additional income from existing sources, redeployment of skilled and experienced humanpower, autonomy in budget and plan preparations, and the power to recruit required staff on the basis of local decisions and available budget. In this regard, it is assumed that these measures will enable citizens and communities to actively participate in development activities and poverty alleviation, and entrench equity and good governance while laying a firm foundation upon which the federal arrangement could rest.

Notwithstanding this, however, a number of shortcomings were experienced, manifested in such things as weak leadership, lack of awareness, inadequate coordination, and entrenchment of defective working systems. It has been only some three years now since grassroots empowerment activities commenced. Wereda and municipal administrations are still in the process of being strengthened. As there are many competing needs, the resource that could be made available for local and grassroots empowerment from the meagre budget at the disposal of weredas and municipalities is rather limited.

Notwithstanding significant improvements in the wereda decentralization, the exercise is confronted by a plethora of drawbacks with regard to adequacy of resources and availability of the services of skilled humanpower as well as management and technical capacity. Bringing about far-reaching changes associated with local and grassroots empowerment through policy reform in Ethiopia is time-consuming (Kurey and Alsop 2004). Therefore, what could be expected from the exercise in the form of achievement at this stage is limited. In this connection, a recent study (CIDA 2005) stated that the devolution of power and authority in governments is not a simple or speedy process, nor should it be. The process takes time and much testing is required particularly in the face of impediments like the reluctance of higher government levels to relinquish parts of their mandate on one hand and the uncertainty of lower levels on how to make use of their devolved mandates on the other.

One could normally expect that the value added of new reforms relating to empowerment should be amply demonstrated in terms of feasible and imaginative planning, a modest increase in the quantity and quality of service delivery, and entrenchment of a relatively efficient expenditure management system. Studies (Kasshaun and Tegegne 2004; Kurey and Alsop 2004) undertaken in some of the regions where wereda decentralization is in full swing have revealed improvements despite constraints encountered. Untied block grants have enabled formulation and implementation of plans with relative ease and convenience as compared to the past. A recent briefing paper (Dom and Mohammed 2006, 2) asserted that from a country-wide perspective, there have been a number of important achievements since the introduction of wereda decentralization despite the numerous challenges that are experienced. The same source also lamented the sluggish pace of the capacity building component of the policy and its implementation, which adversely impacts on subsequent undertakings.

Increased amount of funds at the disposal of wereda governments from a combination of inter-governmental transfers and own revenue has resulted in payment of salaries on time. Recruitment of highly needed humanpower through shifts between approved budget lines is made possible in principle. Moreover, decisions on capital budget and expenditure that previously needed the sanction of higher levels of government have become prerogatives of mainly local governments. With increased autonomy and relatively expanded freedom of action, empowered local administrations are expected to show visible signs of improvement in several respects. These include the taking shape of increased capacity, improved service delivery, better coordination of activities, better planning and growing linkages between local actors and grassroots communities and institutions. To date research pointing to positive results or otherwise is scanty. Some of the literatures available in this area are not conclusive. For example, the DLDP synthesizing study indicates some positive achievements of wereda decentralization in the areas of service delivery, block grant, staff redeployment, financial management pool system while other studies such as the Oxfam study mention that decentralization is not translated into action (Dom and Mohammed 2006). The gap in this regard has to be filled in order to move forward.

2.3.1. Region to Wereda Transfers and Local Revenue

Regions transfer subsidies to local governments to enable the latter to effectively pursue local policy and service delivery. This is done on the basis of a formula which is similar to that used for federal-to-region transfer. The formula consists of population, development level and wereda's own revenue. The 1994 population census figure is used for determining population size. The weights of the parameters vary from region to region but the average were indicated to be population (55%), development level (30%) and own revenue (15%) (Lissane and Mohammed 2005). The federal-based formula has been modified by some regions to consider local expenditure need. The new formula used cost drivers and unit costs by sector. In the Amhara region, regional officials explained that the unit cost approach is effective in enabling weredas to budget for service delivery instead of budgeting for institutions (Dom and Mohammed 2006).

While both the formula and the expenditure based approaches are used to implement the instrument of block grant, there are other transfer instruments used. For instance budget adjustment, contingency assistance, training support, selected cash transfer for capital and operating purposes, food security grants and food aid, asset transfer are some of the different methods used to transfer resources from regions to local governments (Heymans and Mohammed 2004). One significant issue at this juncture is the relative merits of these different instruments, including block grant system, in order to empower local government and improve service delivery at the local level. In particular there is a gap in evaluating the block and non-block grant system of resource transfer from different dimensions. Heymans and Mohammed (2004) suggest consolidating and strengthening the non-block grant transfer without compromising the decentralization objective of the system. This is believed to bring forth greater predictability, more reward for performance, facilities to achieve federal and regional policy goals without compromising wereda-level decentralization (Heymans and Mohammed 2004). Whether this assumption is correct or not needs to be examined and seriously studied

The main source of revenue at local (wereda) level are direct income tax, business tax, rental tax, agricultural land use charges, rural land utilization charges, sales tax, etc. Agriculture being the main driver of most regional economies, it forms an important regional development mechanism (Lissane and Mohammed 2005). There is no clear rule regarding local revenue collection and sharing of local revenue between weredas and regions despite some regions' (e.g. Oromia) claim to have established a revenue-sharing mechanism (Mohammed 2005). Others (e.g. Amhara) have expressed reservation in allowing weredas to retain the revenue generated (Lissane and Mohammed 2005). Weredas therefore continue to collect revenue on behalf of regional governments.

An important issue, however, is the difference among weredas in fiscal and institutional capacity. Fiscally, some weredas, particularly peri-urban weredas, are better off in raising revenue and their reliance on regional subsidies is lesser than remote weredas with limited resource base and hence requiring a higher amount of subsidy. The institutional capacity in collecting revenue also varies greatly. These are indications of the need to identify the institutional gaps in collecting and raising revenues. The issue of capacity, particularly in terms of skilled manpower, also adversely impacted on efficient utilization of public finance, project planning and preparation as revealed by a study undertaken in Oromia and SNNPR (Tesfaye 2000, 45).

2.4. Municipal Decentralization

Though Ethiopia is one of the least urbanized countries in Africa with 15% of urbanization in the year 2005, it has a dramatic pace of urbanization at the rate of 6%. According to the 1994 housing and population survey, it is projected that by the year 2030 it will have an urbanization level of 23%. These urban centers are supposed to be managed by their own municipalities. Municipalities are local governments in smaller and bigger urban centers. These municipalities, however, have remained largely marginalized and experience very weak institutional capacity to lead and support the growth of their urban centers.

A World Bank study conducted in 2001 (Gulyani *et al.* 2001) made a rapid assessment of four municipalities, namely, Bahir Dar, Awassa, Gambella and Dire Dawa. The study found that:

a) Though the functions assigned to municipalities seem to be appropriate, service provision at municipal level is limited; both the coverage and level of services provided are low;

b) Municipalities have very low tax bases with property and business taxes being the most important sources;

c) User charges and fees used by municipalities have no relation to current income and cost since they are based on obsolete legislation;

d) Average collection rates are low reaching 59 % of the planned revenue in Gambella;

e) There are high default rates and arrears;

f) Payment procedures are slow and inconvenient for tax payers;

g) The enforcement mechanisms for revenue collection is poor;

h) There is weak human resource capacity and poor incentive structure;

i) Expenditures are low in absolute size, and

j) There is an increasing trend in the wage bill, which is realized at the expense of capital budgets.

The Ethiopian decentralization scheme, including the constitution of 1995, did not recognize municipalities as an independent entity to which power and resources can be devolved. Some studies, however, point out that the different articles of the constitution allow for the establishment of municipal government by regional states. For example, Article 88 (1) of the constitution which states "... Government shall promote and support the people's self-rule at all levels" allows for municipal Governments (MWUD 1999). Similarly, Article 50 (4), which is about granting of adequate power to the lowest units of Government, and Article 52(2a) which grants powers and functions to States to establish state administrations that best advance self-government are considered to open room for including municipal government in the structure of the federal system. The MWUD (1999) study, while acknowledging the federal constitution to incorporate municipal Governments, emphasizes the need to be more explicit in the regional constitution regarding municipal governments. The arguments put forward to this effect include that an express provision in the regional constitution will: a) insulate municipalities from complete dependence on the State; b) will signify the importance attached by the State to municipalities' role in socio-economic development of the State; c) will amplify their importance in terms of population density, capital investment and public and social services; and d) will avoid practical problems related to the organization of cities, as many cities were given wereda or zonal status which is a lumping together of municipal administration with State government administration (MWUD 1999). The question is to what extent do regions recognize municipalities in their constitutions? The earlier effort to recognize municipalities by regions was the experience of the Oromia, the Amhara and the Tigray regions. The Oromia region issued the municipal authorities and rural kebeles Proclamation no. 4/1993 prior to the issuing of the Federal Constitution. The Amhara region has issued two pieces of municipal legislations, namely: the organization of Bahir Dar as a special zone and the definition of its duties and responsibilities in regulation no. 3/1995 and the reorganization of urban wereda administration and municipalities and the definition of their duties and responsibilities in a of regulation 1997. Tigray region enacted municipalities administration proclamation no. 21/1997. Under this law municipalities collected taxes, charges and fees. The details, however, were provided in the 1971 regulation (Jemal 2000). These regional legislations were found out to be inadequate (MWUD 1999). Recently there have been several attempts to correct the deficiencies and empower the municipalities.

Beginning from 2001, municipalities have started to be revived in Ethiopia. This period corresponds with the second wave of decentralization, namely, wereda decentralization. Many regional governments resorted to reforming their municipalities by enacting municipal legislations that define the legislative system that clarifies the position of municipalities within the decentralized governance. The Amhara, Oromia, Tigray and SNNP regions have enacted municipal proclamations. The proclamations define the governance structure and the various roles and responsibilities of municipalities. Regarding governance structure, most regions have opted for the Council-Mayor system. The governance organ includes the City Council and the Speaker of the Council, the Mayor and the Mayor's committee, and the Manager of the Municipal Services. The Council-Mayor system provides executive leadership in the mayor who is often elected and serves as a chair and political heavy weight (Minas 2003). The Mayor has both governance and management responsibilities. In order for the cities to benefit from professional management, councils elect a city manager on merit basis. The city, among others, has the capacity to issue laws and regulations, establish the executive organs, establish judicial and policy organs.

In general, cities in each region are graded on the basis of some criteria, from advanced cities (over 100,000 for regional capitals) to medium and emerging towns. For example, in the Amhara region, the city organization has the structure of city administration, municipalities and emerging towns (ANRS 2003). Each region has designated towns in which the reform could be implemented. Currently the number of reforming towns has increased.

In the current reform, urban administrations have two types of functions: state and municipal. State functions, which include education, health, trade and industry, are financed from regional transfers while municipal functions such as solid waste collection, sewerage, street lighting, etc., are to be self-financed from own revenue generated from such sources as land lease, housing rental income, service taxes, service charges, etc. These functions exist as parallel systems and they entail a separate financial system. One of the issues in municipal decentralization is the integration of municipal and state functions so as to have a consolidated financial system. It is indicated that the Amhara region has taken steps towards the integration of the municipal and state functions (Hegedus, Mohammed and Peterson 2006). In this regard it is important to understand whether integration would advance municipal causes or not as systematic studies along this line are lacking.

2.5 Municipal Finance

Prior to the year 2001, municipalities depended on local resources as there was no regular grant from either the federal government or regional government. The revenue from these sources was very small and even declined because of tariff stagnation (Jemal 2000).

Since 2001, a different funding framework has been emerging for urban areas. Urban areas receive transfers from regional governments as agency payments for the performance of regional state functions, but municipalities are also expected to be self-financing for their municipal functions through different income sources (land leases, housing rental incomes, tax for services provided by the municipality, service usage charge, small local penalties, issuing licenses). Hence municipalities generate their finance from two sources: block grant and own revenues. According to wereda/city government benchmarking study, block grant is the major source of budgeted revenue constituting 55.3% of the total (MoFED 2005). Own revenues of municipalities account for 44.7% of total revenue. In terms of expenditure, local roads and administrative expenses form the major municipal function expenditure with a combined share of 68%. With regard to state function expenditure, education expenditure has the highest share with a share of 39.5 % (MoFED 2005).

Municipal finance was recently studied by MUUD in cooperation with GTZ and Urban Institute. The report for SNNPR, which is based on a study of four urban local governments (Awassa, Dilla, Sodo and Arbaminch), noted the low revenue of cities due to outdated tariffs and rates. The tax collection rate in the region is between 70-80% on average in the four municipalities. The sources of revenue include land tax, building tax, livestock, trade tax, vehicle road tax, business and professional fee, other tax income, lease income, rental income, service charge, administrative fee and others. The revenue composition indicates that land tax is the most important source of revenue for all urban local governments. On the expenditure side, recurrent expenditures are higher than capital, with salaries being the most important contributing item for recurrent expenditure. The City administration proclamation of the regional state (Proclamation no. 52/2002) empowers city administrations to set, determine and revise the level of tariff and rates though the regulation issued later (Regulation no. 13/2003) reduced the powers given to local governments (MWUD 2006).

The above study is an indication of the fact that though municipalities are being recognized in the regional proclamations, there is still a need to fully empower cities and provide financial autonomy which may require setting consistent and transparent regulations and by-laws dealing with different dimensions of municipal finance.

3. Impacts of Decentralization

3.1. Decentralization and Service Delivery

One of the objectives of the recent wereda decentralization drive is stated as enabling local governments to provide quality and efficient services at decentralized levels through promoting good governance, enhancing organizational effectiveness, and improving humanpower capacity (Mohammed Seid 2006). To achieve these objectives, interventions in the form of institutional rearrangement, manning/staffing and training, fiscal transfer and revenue enhancement, local planning and control, entrenching grassroots participation, and standard service and equipment supply were deemed essential (Worku 2004). It is widely recognized that in the absence of improvement in service delivery, it is hardly possible to tackle the entrenched and prevalent problem of poverty and lack of income affecting wider sections of the population thereby impeding endeavors to embark on socio-economic development.

In this connection, it is worthy to note that the perception with regard to service provision and concomitant recourse mechanisms is determined by the extent of the reliance of the community on government structures, the existence and contribution of alternative private agents of service delivery at local and community levels, and the presence of avenues for expressing dissatisfaction with delivery of services. In the Ethiopian case, studies (Van der Loop 2002) indicate that there are few alternative providers and/or producers of services and infrastructure, particularly for urban areas, where provision of public services are more or less undertaken in the same way. Nevertheless, the level of public service provision in urban centers follows some kind of urban hierarchy in the form of a strong primate city, intermediate urban areas and small towns in descending order.

Ethiopia has been practicing a unitary form of government characterized by de-concentrated and delegated type of decentralization in all fields, including service delivery. A devolved form of decentralization is a recent phenomenon that accompanied the 1991 regime change that ushered in the federal arrangement. Prior to this, sub-national level entities and actors were required to unconditionally comply with decisions and directives issued from the center on matters concerning socio-economic activities and service delivery at the local levels (Kumera 2006). Since 1991, Ethiopia has embarked on a new socio-economic and political direction that laid a favorable ground for a relatively improved and decentralized service delivery. This is commensurate with endeavors associated with adjustment of economic policy and rehabilitation of structures through a series of reform measures (Hamdok 2003). The reforms were aimed at limiting the role of the state in the economy through privatization and inducing government to focus on strategic and regulatory functions while at the same time shifting responsibilities pertaining to service delivery to sub-national governments (Befekadu 1994).

Following the inauguration of the FDRE and the coming on the scene of the incumbent constitution in 1995, significant variations with regard to the delivery capacity of the different regions of the Ethiopian federation have been observed (Word Bank 2002).

It is claimed that improvement in the provision of public services using the decentralized governance approach is one of the major objectives of the wereda decentralization program. In turn, improvement in the quality and mode of service delivery is expected to boost and enhance socio-economic development efforts (Mohammed 2006).

Public service delivery at the local level in the major regions where wereda decentralization is taking effect is structured at two levels: the first is centered in the wereda capital towns where administrative bodies and service-oriented sector offices are located, the second is found at the grassroots/community level in the kebeles and other units below them. In relation to the decentralization drive associated with public service delivery, activities are performed on the basis of locally identified and agreed on priorities and by considering plans and budget approved by relevant bodies in the pertinent levels of government. Different sector offices organized under the wereda administrations that are engaged in service delivery include Finance and Economic Development, Agriculture, Education, Health, Water Supply, Rural Roads, and Security and Justice, among others. Sector offices dealing with education, health, water supply and roads have direct contacts with the community and exercise both downward (to the community) and upward (to higher tiers) accountability. This takes place mainly in the formal sense and to a lesser degree in actual fact particularly as regards downward accountability. Accountability to constituencies at the grassroots level is actualized through their kebele field offices, which play considerable roles in coordinating activities and mobilizing community participation (Kumera 2006).

Education and health offices coordinate and provide educational and health services at schools and health centers and health posts, respectively, in different kebeles and sub-kebeles. Water and rural roads offices provide services through direct contacts with communities and grassroots units without necessarily having field agents and branch offices at that level. Offices of agriculture provide mainly extension services and coordinate community activities by making use of development agents deployed to serve in the kebeles (Kumera 2006). Services provided in the fields of education, health, water supply, agricultural extension, and rural roads stand out as critical fields of engagement of the concerned sector offices. Activities in this regard are considered to be crucial in the realization of poverty reduction efforts and associated developmental goals. Given that education is crucial for enhancing social and economic development, educational services were provided at wereda and lower levels even prior to the recent wereda decentralization drive. Services in the fields of education, health, rural roads and water supply were under the jurisdiction of pertinent zonal departments prior to decentralization whereas the situation was reversed making weredas responsible for these services after the commencement of wereda decentralization.

Wereda education offices discharge their responsibilities in coordination with Kebele Education and Training Boards (KETBs) and Parent-Teacher Associations (PTAs) operating at grassroots/community levels. Community members/parents actively participate in school management by involving in decision making processes. Following the deepening of the decentralization drive that commenced in 2001/2002, formal mechanisms for strengthening community participation in educational activities unfolded.

The establishment of KETBs and PTAs was based on the guidelines of the Federal Ministry of Education, which are adopted by the regional governments that have embarked on wereda decentralization. The guidelines underlined the need for strengthening the relationship between parents and schools, promoting educational programs by facilitating conditions for effective teaching and learning interface, and entrenching a more participatory and disciplined environment in the teaching-learning process (Kassahun and Tegegne 2004). The guidelines make it mandatory for each school to establish PTA and KETB. The role of PTAs is advisory and limited to working closely with schools on issues of student and staff discipline and other matters. PTAs are accountable to KETBs, which are charged with the task of managing kebele schools.

Wereda health offices oversee the activities of health centers, health stations and health posts that are often located in wereda towns, accessible spots, and villages respectively. Health centers are often found in wereda towns and serve as mini-hospitals and referrals for health posts whereas health posts are facilities placed in rural kebeles at village/kebele levels. Kebele health posts serve as first instance units where community members in the villages receive services as the need arises (Kumera 2006). Health posts are established to provide basic health services by way of prevention and treatment in a manner that does not call for big investment as regards software and hardware inputs (Kassahun and Tegegne 2004). The focus of health posts is mostly on prevention and training of selected community members on basics and preliminaries of personal, household and environmental hygiene and care. They are also charged with the task of providing medical assistance for minor ailments, pre- and post-natal treatment, reproductive health, and child delivery (Kassahun and Tegegne 2004).

At the kebele level, health teams are elected from among the ranks of residents in the villages that are designated as sub-kebeles. Elected members representing sub-kebeles constitute kebele health teams. The kebele health teams work closely with trained health workers who serve as hubs that create rapport between kebeles and weredas with regard to health matters. Kebele health teams are charged with the responsibility of following up health hazards (outbreak of epidemics) and report such and similar developments to kebele administrations, mobilize community resources (labor, material, and funds) to make beneficiaries share the burden of government expenditure, and sensitize constituencies on causes and consequences of health hazards (Kassahun and Tegegne 2004).

At the level of official policy and practices that are in the process of being attempted, the role of decentralized service delivery at the local level appears to have been clearly articulated. It goes without saying, however, that drives aiming at improving service delivery call for enhanced capacity in terms of availability of skilled and experienced personnel, existence of able and committed leadership, adequacy of logistical, financial and infrastructural amenities (Kumera 2006), and prevalence of feasible and imaginative planning mechanisms and procedures. Nevertheless, efficient and quality delivery of public services in Ethiopia, including in the so-called relatively developed and advanced major regions is more often constrained by paucity of the aforementioned resources. Such drawbacks are compounded by the incidence of frequent turnover of experienced officials and experts/functionaries either as a result of transfers or dismissals and resignations accruing from a variety of reasons, including politico-administrative variables. It is also stated that apart from deficits pertaining to technical expertise at the disposal of decentralized units of governance, weak and defective institutional arrangements (Tegegne 2000) could be taken as contributory factors impeding positive outcomes of decentralization in terms of service delivery.

At this juncture, it would be worthwhile to say a few words in relation to accountability of service providers on the one hand and the rights of service users on the other. A number of recent studies have noted problems that are associated with these issues. In spite of the fact that the legal basis for empowering service users is currently in place, it appears that there is still a long way to go before this objective could be realized. Mismatch between supply and demand as well as facility constraints are identified as some of the factors that undermine both delivery and provider accountability in several cases (Tegegne, Assefa, Kassahun and Meheret 2004). A study conducted by the Institute of Educational Research (IER) (IER 2002), Addis Ababa University, brought to light that among the reasons weakening the accountability of service providers are lack of information on how and where to lodge complaints on the part of users, the absence of institutional mechanisms for redress, disillusionment with regard to the performance and effectiveness of the national integrity system comprising the courts, the police, legislatures, and other watchdog agencies.

It could be argued that, in principle, the sanctioning of decentralized service delivery can facilitate closer community and user oversight and scrutiny with regard to the performance of service providers thereby increasing chances for controlling abuse (Kassahun and Tegegne 2004). However, the fact that service providers at the local government level lack the necessary capacity to induce participatory processes undermines accountability in several respects, including service delivery. Since grassroots communities and their associations lack sufficient awareness with regard to the specifics of the on-going decentralization drives, prospects for entrenching accountability of service providers are low (Kassahun and Tegegne 2004). Such a dismal situation is compounded by the absence of strong organizations and networks as the major underpinnings of associations of service users (Kassahun and Tegegne 2004). Paucity of robust civil society organizations in Ethiopia that could actively engage in ensuring the empowerment of members expressed in holding government and service providers accountable is a major shortcoming in this regard. This is compounded by the strong presence and intrusion of the ruling party and its affiliate political entrepreneurs in all spheres of life thereby rendering the realization of legitimate claims and aspirations of citizens in terms of participation and decision making ineffective. It is evident that the prevalence of firm party and bureaucratic control as is the case in Ethiopia nurtures a favorable environment for the entrenchment of a top-down modality of operation thereby neutralizing endeavors towards taking advantage of decentralization measures in a manner that could strengthen empowerment and participatory processes. Notwithstanding this, however, various committees representing communities have been formed. In addition to their role in raising financial and other community contributions, these committees are active in ensuring that service delivery operational policies are applied (Dom and Mohammed 2006, 8-9).

Hence it is suggested (Muir 2005) that prevalent shortcomings could be ameliorated through recourse to a variety of measures such as inducing active participation in planning and budgeting processes pertaining to service delivery, introducing a system of service delivery report cards, facilitating informed and active involvement and legitimate representation of civil society organizations, among others.

3.2. Decentralization and Socio-Economic Development

The Ethiopian Government's drive to bring socio-economic development in the country is reflected in the various strategies, policies and sector development programs it has developed. Sector development programs on education, health, roads, agriculture, food security, energy and water resources are clear indications of the government's intention to improve the living standards of the people. The extent to which these initiatives have been assisted, promoted or facilitated by a decentralized structure needs to be examined. Since the decentralization drive, regions have been empowered to plan and execute development programs on their own initiative. The block grant is the main instruments to this effect. Not only do regions prepare their own five-year and annual plans, but they are also the main partners in the implementation of various sector programs. For instance, in agriculture, while the Federal Ministry of Agriculture is responsible for policy formulation and strategy design at the national level, the regional Bureaus of Agriculture are responsible for on-the ground implementation of policies and strategies and development programs (extension packages) (Getachew 2001). Regarding resources destined for the development of agriculture, the share of regions has increased from a little more than 33% in 1993/94 to 70% in 1996/97 (Getachew 2001).

The most visible impact of decentralization on socio-economic development is in the area of infrastructural development: rural road, education and health services. Rural road construction is an important instrument of rural development. Rural road construction is the responsibility of Regional Governments. Increase in the volume of investment and the length of rural road constructed is a clear benefit of decentralization. The rural road in Ethiopia has grown from 10,680 km in 1997 to 18,406 km in 2005 (see appendix 3). This shows a 72% change in the growth of rural roads. With regard to education, the administration of primary and secondary education has been decentralized and as a result local administrations are responsible to deliver these services (see above). Studies indicate that gross enrollment ratio in primary and secondary schools has increased and gender gap has declined (Getachew 2001). While this may be an achievement of the Regional Governments in raising the service coverage, the quality of the service leaves much to be desired. The very high teacher/student ratio affects the quality of education.

With regard to health, the regional Health Bureaus have assumed greater authority and responsibility in the organization, planning, capacity building, coordination, implementation and monitoring of the health care system in their own regional administrations (see above). The health expenditure as a share of the total regional expenditure amounts to 90% of the total consolidated expenditure on health (Getachew 2001). There is also an increase in the number of health facilities such as health posts and health centers at the regional level. Despite this, the health sector is faced with some difficulties. In particular, the public utilization of health facilities is less than the population growth.

One important aspect of socio-economic development is private sector development. In the 'developmental state' era the private sector was considered to be too weak to lead development. The State was considered to be capable of engineering economic and social transformation. Following the growing disappointment with the developmental State and particularly its inability to deliver services and cope with economic crisis, structural adjustment and liberalization introduced a new era in which the role of the State was reduced (Helmsing cited in Wolday *et al.* 2005). The private sector thrives in a situation where all its determinants are in place. Conducive policies and reforms that have implications for private sector development are among the enabling environment required for thriving private sector. Decentralization is one of the many reforms that have significant implications for private sector development[2]. As decentralization devolves power, autonomy and resources to local government, it enables local authorities to exercise power and create a conducive situation for private sector development. One area that has significant impact on private sector development in Ethiopia is the devolution of the administration of natural resources, especially land. As a result, private investors are expected to negotiate the terms and conditions of acquiring land with regional governments once they have acquired their licenses from the federal government (Ethiopian investment office) (Getachew 2001). Hence the speed and modality of land allocation by regional governments have significant implication for private sector development, particularly those involved in productive sectors (agriculture and industry). In addition, the infrastructural base which is partly the responsibility of regional governments also affects investment decisions of investors.

While regional Investment Bureaus in all regions approve private investment projects, the regional differences in investment projects could be partly attributed, among others, to differences in infrastructural base, ease and convenience of obtaining land, all of which have relation with the decentralization drive of different regions.

---

[2] The other policies and reforms that have implications for private sector development include the SDPRP, industrial development strategy, financial sector reform, governance reform, civil service reform, judicial reform, etc.

3.3. Decentralization and Poverty Reduction

In the international literature, decentralization is receiving increased attention as a potential tool in the fight against poverty. The decentralization and poverty link is assumed to follow two channels: political and economic (Jutting *et al.* 2004). Political or democratic decentralization offers citizens the possibility of increased participation in local decision making processes. Improved representation leads to better access to local public services and social security schemes reducing vulnerability and insecurity (Jutting *et al.* 2004). Since political decentralization also allows for power sharing, it creates grounds for political consensus and stability which in turn presents a foundation for the poor to build up their life and begin investing. The economic channel of decentralization will impact on poverty through increased efficiency and better targeting of services (Jutting *et al.* 2004). Both will improve the situation of the poor in access to services. The impact of decentralization on poverty is mediated by two sets of conditions: background and process. The former relates to country setting, capacity of local actors, political power structure, and social institutions while the latter refers to willingness and ability to carry out reforms, transparent and participative process, elite capture and corruption and policy coherence and process (Jutting *et al.* 2004).

Poverty reduction is the core agenda of Ethiopia's development strategy. The country prepared SDPRP that run from 2001-2006. The SDPRP indicated that the strategy of poverty reduction in Ethiopia rests on four pillars: ADLI, Justice System and Civil Service Reform, decentralization and empowerment and capacity building in public and private sectors. PASDEP, which emphasizes growth to reduce poverty, acknowledges that initiatives that started under SDPRP I will continue (PASDEP 2005). The above indicates that though the initial motives of decentralization in Ethiopia do not have much link with poverty reduction, recent developments have embraced poverty reduction as part of the decentralization effort. Local governments in Ethiopia are bestowed with a power of socio-economic development including poverty reduction.

Despite this, studies on the impact of decentralization on poverty are limited. De Jong, Loquai and Soiri (1999) attempted to see the link between poverty reduction and decentralization by focusing on local governments (weredas). The study was based on desk analysis and short filed work in three districts of Bugna, Awassa and Kewot, and Addis Ababa. The general conclusion of the study was that local governments have very limited added value in poverty reduction. The studied communities viewed decentralization as not benefiting them in terms of space for participation and designing improved poverty reduction strategies.

More specifically, the study found out that wereda and kebele administrations are not truly operational because of a number of constraints such as lack of autonomy, lack of accountability and representation, lack of meaningful participation of local community, problem of resource mobilization and human capital constraint. In addition, it was also found that the federal political arrangement does not provide population with a means of participation, local governments do not carry out poverty reduction strategies and the agricultural extension and credit system do not assist the poorest sectors of the society (de Jong, Loquai and Soiri 1999).

An OECD study has attempted to look at the link between poverty and decentralization for 19 countries including Ethiopia (Jutting *et al.* 2004). Based on the results, four performance categories of decentralization's impact on poverty were defined: i) positive, ii) somewhat positive, iii) somewhat negative, and iv) negative. According to the study, Ethiopia belongs to a group of nine countries which are grouped as 'somewhat negative' (Jutting *et al.* 2004). The countries are grouped as being generally unstable, emerging from civil war or ethnic conflict. The overriding objective of decentralization in these countries is political stability and maintenance of central control and decentralization is not designed for its benefits in terms of democratization, greater responsiveness to local needs, and community participation which are the three dimensions of poverty reduction (Jutting *et al.* 2004). This contrasts with the characteristics of countries labeled as 'positive performers' or 'somewhat positive performers' whose rational for decentralization has been economic and the reform has been inspired by the desire to improve social, economic, and political conditions in the contexts of democratization, community participation and poverty reduction (Jutting *et al.* 2004).

De Jong, Loquai and Soiri's study and the OECD case study pre-date 2001, which witnessed wereda decentralization. It is quite normal to assume that poverty reduction efforts might have improved after wereda decentralization. Edegilign's (2006) thesis has a mixed reaction to such claims. Edegilign (2006) examined the delivery of pro-poor services in one Yem special wereda in an attempt to see whether decentralization has helped the poor in terms of improving services. Pro-poor services are meant to be health, education, rural water supply and agricultural extension. The study found an increasing trend in the physical access to basic services in the wereda. Hence increase in the number of primary schools, enrollment rates, health posts, preventive health care services, drinking water, households covered by improved agricultural inputs were registered. The thesis also acknowledged the existence of community structures such as Parent Teachers Association (PTA), Kebele Education and Training Board (KETB), health committees, health extension workers that may have impacts on increasing the coverage of the basic services. On the other hand improvements in physical availability are not matched by improved quality of health and education supplies and qualified teachers (Edegilign 2006). In addition, despite the increasing physical coverage there is still a high unmet demand for pro-poor services in the wereda.[3] The thesis further underlines that the achievements in some services (e.g. water) are mostly associated with sector office's and NGO's effort and not due to the response given by the local administration to local demands. In this thesis, though an increased coverage of services is noted, it is difficult to isolate the impacts of decentralization on service coverage. The increased coverage could have different sources such as budget increase, population increase or more demand for services, etc. A clear attribution of pro-poor service coverage to decentralization remains to be studied. In addition, in order to study the impact of decentralization on poverty it is important to understand the determinants of pro-poor decentralization outcome such as ability and willingness to carry reform (financial resources at local level, local human capacity, political commitment at the national level, donor involvement and support, transparent and participative process, role of civil society, elite capture and corruption, etc.)

3.4. Decentralization, Citizen Empowerment, Participation and Planning

Citizen participation and voice relate to involvement of communities in committee undertakings pertaining to service delivery. Communities in the four major regions in question undertake different activities by participating in the various committees: Parent-Teacher Associations/Kebele Education and Trainings Boards, Water User and Irrigation Groups, Health Teams, Social Courts, Cooperative Societies, Environmental Protection Groups, etc. With a fair degree of technical assistance of expertise at the disposal of wereda sector offices, the different teams and committees undertake their respective tasks that are mainly commensurate with the needs of their constituencies.

Formal arrangements and official rhetoric aside, however, the issue of ensuring citizen participation is bedeviled by several constraints. It is argued that people at the grassroots level so far have failed to perceive the benefit of decentralization in terms of space being provided for genuine and meaningful participation and alleviation of their lots through intervention of regional and local authorities (Tegegne and Kassahun 2004). This is owing to the fact that local authorities often fail to deliver what is expected of them due to several constraints. These relate to the limited pool of capable individuals available to fill vacant positions in the public sector, prevalence of patronage rendering appointed officials to be more responsive to government /party preferences to

---

[3] For instance 72% of the wereda residents have no access to safe drinking water.

the detriment of legitimate demands and aspirations of citizens, diminished influence of elected representatives on official decisions, lack of resources at the disposal of elected bodies like kebeles, and discouragement by officialdom restraining citizen outspokenness (Kurey and Alsop 2005).

The Ministry of Capacity Building of GOE (2004) affirmed that currently there is no forum that brings civil society actors and government to undertake dialogue on how to engage with each other. The prevalence of such state of affairs is indicative of the fact that citizens' voices and aspirations largely remain unrealized as a result of a near total absence of interface and mutual engagement.

Notwithstanding the several improvements relating to citizen voice and participation witnessed since the 1991 regime change in Ethiopia, limitations emanating from a host of shortcomings have rendered attempts towards transforming citizen empowerment ineffective (Tegegne, Assefa, Kassahun and Meheret 2004). Prevalent state of affairs pertaining to independence of CSOs, their role in conflict prevention and resource management, and influence on policy making and program formulation is marginal (Tegegne, Assefa, Kassahun and Meheret 2004). The absence and ineffectiveness of citizen voice is illustrated by a World Bank study (World Bank 2002) regarding the exclusion of communities from participating in planning and budget processes, and that need identification is often subordinated to national and regional sectoral plans thereby diminishing the extent of effectiveness of citizen voice. The same source also asserts that no indicative budget is taken in to discussions with communities, which are in effect asked to list their wishes rather than determine their priorities. The reconciliation of such wishes with the wereda budgets often takes place without involving the concerned frontline offices and functionaries (World Bank 2002).

With some modifications and insignificant improvements that are witnessed following wereda decentralization, the overall situation in this regard remains essentially unaltered. To do justice to the objectives of the recent decentralization moves, it could be justifiably argued that capacity limitations affecting both local level administrations and grassroots actors account for failures in bringing speedy transformation of entrenched dispositions and practices. At this juncture, it is also worthy to note that women's needs and inputs are very poorly reflected in community planning processes. The same applies to the situation of traditionally marginalized groups like pastoralists and the youth. In addition to the aforementioned, several groups among citizens and actors at the grassroots level have little or no information regarding the unfolding of policy processes, contents of policies, and their rights and roles associated with measures of empowerment. Factors that render citizen voice ineffective are, therefore, compounded by lack of information and awareness on the ramifications of what is unfolding in terms of empowerment.

Drawbacks experienced since the initiation of the recent decentralization drive are brought to light by a survey conducted recently (MoFED 2005). According to the survey, newly empowered local units of government that accommodate representatives of grassroots communities are constrained by limited discretionary powers in expenditure assignments forced on them through budget guidelines provided by regional authorities. In the worst cases, weredas do not plan their budget and simply wait for the actual release of disbursement. Hence there is a need for budget planning capacity of wereda governments on the one hand, and adherence to the principle of united block grant scheme on the part of regional officials on the other. Reporting problems relating to the loan/ grant portion of budgeted revenue were also uncovered by the survey. This was attributed to lack of awareness on the part of wereda staff regarding the loan /grant component of their budgeted revenue. The level of consultation taking place between weredas and communities in the surveyed samples on such issues as strategic plans, budgets and changes in service delivery, however, was found to be reasonable. The act of depriving local governments of discretionary powers constraining their empowerment is manifested in the form of consultations that often assume postures of providing guidelines and instructions. Such a disposition cannot qualify as a good approach for ensuring citizen voice.

The impact of all of the above-mentioned positive developments on grassroots development is reportedly constrained by, (i) inadequate resources, both human and material, particularly at the wereda level, (ii) limited time since the whole decentralization process has commenced anew (only some 3 years back), (iii) narrow understanding of the correct meaning and scope of empowerment, and (iv) significant reliance on the traditional mode of representation through elected council members, and by resorting to mass mobilization and mass consultation. The decentralization effort, therefore, has yet to trickle down to kebele and community levels with a view to engendering empowerment at the grassroots level.

The process of considering citizens' voice and preferences in planning processes have been formally initiated following the commencement of the recent decentralization drive. Formally and officially, local (wereda) governments currently use new bottom-up guidelines in their planning and budgeting exercises (CIDA 2005). Prior to the unfolding of the wereda decentralization scheme, the exclusion of communities from participating in planning and budgeting processes was commonplace and that priorities were subordinated to national and regional sectoral plans thereby totally disregarding the needs and preferences of citizens (World Bank 2002). Another study (MoFED 2005) affirmed this assertion by stating "no indicative budget is taken into discussion with communities, which are in effect asked to list their wishes rather than determine their priorities".

Changes experienced following wereda decentralization underline the fact that the planning process commences at kebele (sub-wereda) level through consultation with lower units (sub-kebeles and village teams) the outcomes of which qualify as kebele consolidated plans. Budgeted activities to be undertaken in a given fiscal year specify the amount of expenditure to be covered through government allocations and community contributions (finance, labor, material) subject to the approval and final decision of cabinets and councils of local (wereda) governments. It is worthy to note here that the recent decentralization scheme has initiated a process of giving voice, with regard to their needs and preferences, to citizens and communities (Kassahun and Tegegne 2004; Kurey and Alsop 2005).

3.5. Decentralization and the Environment

It is now accepted that natural resources, like service provision and local development, can benefit from the redistribution of central government authority (Larson 2002). This is mainly because the goals of decentralization coincide with the needs of effective natural resource management. The latter requires the involvement of local people to identify and prioritize environmental problems, to have a greater sense of ownership of decisions made locally, such as rules for resource use, efficient resource allocation and lower information cost (Larson 2002).

Studies that link decentralization to environmental protection in Ethiopia are scanty and very limited. Degarge, Befekadu and Wossenu (2000) attempted to look at decentralization and environmental protection in the two regions of Addis Ababa and Benishangul-Gumuz in the year 2000. The findings were presented under the topics of successful DNRM and successful environmental protection. Under the previous heading, it was found out that regions do not have enough capacity to manage natural resources, as they have limited authority and resource capacity. The absence of a structure for local community participation, incentive scheme and lack of coordination of partners are mentioned as constraining decentralized resource management. Fragmented and uncoordinated decision-making, lack of accountable and responsive management of resources and lack of adequate monitoring are other constraints mentioned in the study. Some success stories were also noted. In Benishangul, for example, the Sherkole refugee camp is mentioned as having a sound system of responsibility and accountability in managing resources and the appointment of community forest guard in particular. Though this study is useful to bring the issue to the surface, the findings do not fully establish the link between decentralization and resource management or environmental protection. It is very critical to examine and analyze where and how the goals of natural resource management meet the goals of decentralization?

4. Implementation of the Decentralization Policy

According to Parry (1997, 212), a strong obstacle in implementing decentralization policies in developing countries is the lack of political will on the part of central governments to relinquish decision making authority to lower levels of government. It is also argued that successful decentralization does not necessarily mean achievement of results in the absence of equity and quality assurance measures (Abebe 2000). Successful decentralization requires that the central government should define the duties and powers of each level of government and institution that are involved in decentralized activities, and determine the goods and services to be provided and the most effective level at which they could be provided better (ibid.).

Decentralized governance at the local level characterized by a set of reforms such as intergovernmental transfer in the form of untied block grants, redeployment of skilled and experienced personnel to weredas, and autonomy in terms of activity and budget planning and staff recruitment within limits of available and approved means have entailed the prevalence of a relatively enabling environment as compared to previous state of affairs. Several improvements with regard to planning, budget allocation, priority setting, and expenditure autonomy were experienced since then. These are expected to "progressively ameliorate inadequacies and constraints that hitherto impeded smooth progress" (Kassahun and Tegegne 2004) of undertakings including service delivery at the local level.

4.1. Decentralized Governance and Capacity

In this section, a brief appraisal of the implementation of the major components of the recent decentralization program in view of the brief experience since its commencement is made.

Institutional capacity is defined as the ability to set goals, anticipate needs, make informed decisions, and attract and manage resources in order to meet those goals (Parry 1997). The issue of capacity as it relates to local governments is a matter that needs to be examined from different angles and perspectives. In this regard, UNCDF (2003) rightly states that it is by no means self-evident that local governments know the kinds of capacity needed for running their activities. According to Mulualem (2001, 68-69), in order to be competent, agencies must be well-equipped with adequately trained personnel and logistical resources. This is affirmed by other studies (Rondinelli 1993, World Bank 1997) which underlined that availability and full utilization of highly trained and motivated staff are of paramount importance for achieving success in any institution building process.

Hence there is a need to introduce a supply-driven scheme that provides them with a menu of essential and basic capacity building activities. It was noted that some of the problems observed in all regions of Ethiopia include weak administrative capacity, shortage of technical humanpower, weak institutionalization characteristic of regional governments, and poor logistical resources (Tegegne 2000). The prevalence of these drawbacks was also highlighted in other studies (Meheret 2002) which indicate that the dearth of trained personnel, weak revenue base, heavy financial dependence on upper echelons of government, low level of awareness of local communities on the roles and functions of a responsible local government, among others, are constraining factors with regard to the entrenchment of democratic local government units. Among the more serious problems faced in the process of implementing the wereda decentralization program are: lack of an integrated system of procedure in service delivery, paucity of efficient organizational structure, absence of a vibrant system for popular participation, and non-existence of a well coordinated and locally adapted working system for planning and execution of budgetary decisions (Ministry of Capacity Building 2004). These relate to the existence of overlapping mandates, low level of popular participation, inadequacy of the existing organizational structure that fails to clearly define the roles of institutional actors, and failure in adapting procedures and working systems to realities peculiar to the different localities.

In order to fully appreciate the pace and level of the on-going initiative, it is worthwhile to look into the situation of the major components of the decentralization program, albeit briefly.

One of the most important assumptions regarding devolution of power and responsibility to local governments was that experts and professionals deployed in the weredas would assist in bolstering coordination and technical service. This was introduced as an important component of DLDP by recognizing problems associated with shortage of skilled humanpower at lower levels of government, which posed the greatest challenge in institutionalizing a properly functioning local government in the country (Meheret 2002). Contrary to prior assumptions and expectations, deployment of skilled staff that could serve in local governments and enhance efforts towards the realization of stated objectives did not materialize owing to the following reasons (Kassahun and Tegegne 2004):

- Aggregate number of staff deployed was less than required to implement the mandate of wereda sector offices;

- Budgetary constraints led to shortfall in recruiting the required number of qualified staff;

- Lack of appropriate candidates who could fill vacant technical posts even if the budget were available;

- Lack of interest on the part of eligible candidates owing to low pay scales and poor incentive packages;

- Prevalence of arbitrary intra and inter-departmental transfer of existing staff thereby resulting in discontinuity and undermining of institutional memory.

In the face of the aforementioned, local governments are left with no option other than continuing with their traditional reliance on upper tiers that are expected to supply experts that provide the former with technical assistance (Joint Support Mission, Aide Memoir 2005). The predicament of local governments in terms of benefiting from the services of skilled and experienced humanpower is also compounded by frequent turnover and attrition (*ibid.*). Provisioning of quality and efficient services is also negatively affected as a result of post-1991 developments and policy directions. This is owing to the according of primacy to ethnicity and language in a manner that is detrimental to meritocracy, which is relegated to the background thereby adversely affecting performance in the civil service (Tesfaye 2000, 60-61).

Despite improvements following the introduction of the block grant scheme, the revenue of weredas originating from transfers and "own" revenue sources still remains meager and falls below the level required to implement planned activities. Most of the revenue originating from intergovernmental transfers and local sources is used to cover recurrent costs (mainly salaries) thereby leaving little room for capital expenditures (Muir 2005).

4.2. Institution Building in the Public Sector

It is to be recalled that power is formally devolved to nine regional state governments and two city administrations following Ethiopia's adoption of a federal form of government in 1991. This set the tone for the establishment of new regional and local government institutions that are charged with the responsibility of undertaking different activities that are in line with their respective mandates (Tegegne and Kassahun 2004). Legislative, executive and judicial branches of government were established at the federal, regional and local levels. In line with the federal constitution, state governments adopted constitutions that accord powers and responsibilities to local governments, whose elected councils serve as the supreme decision making authority. Below the local government level, associations of grassroots communities, *kebeles*, with their elected councils, play similar roles as the ones in the upper (wereda) echelons but at a lower level. Official policy and rhetoric aside, it is worthy to note that the omnipresence of the ruling party and its functionaries in all spheres and at all levels has made the organs to adhere to its organizational programs and preferences. In other words, the Ethiopian decentralization drive is centrally controlled in spite of the fact that it appears to be a form of political devolution.

Institution building has been mentioned as one of the major concerns of the government in its drive to usher in a system of decentralized governance and deal with prevalent problems of poverty. The Ethiopian Poverty Reduction Strategy Paper (PRSP) defines capacity building as a systematic combination of human resources, working systems, and institutions that could enable the country to achieve its development objectives (MoFED 2002). The strategy document emphasizes the need for building the institutional capacity of public, private and civil society organizations so as to enable them to play their respective roles effectively in a manner that could contribute towards the realization of stated development goals (MoFED 2002). Studies (Meheret 2002; World Bank 2001) indicate, however, that power is not sufficiently devolved as stipulated in the pertinent policy and legal provisions. What is observed at the local level is deconcentration rather than devolution. This is corroborated by the fact that the ruling party that is prone to upward accountability dominates the entire realm of political governance at all levels (Tegegne and Kassahun 2004).

In summary, the unfolding of the decentralization process has entailed the creation of institutions of governance in the public sector at various levels (national, regional, local, and grassroots) though this is not well translated into the non-state sectors (see below).

5. Other Issues of Decentralization

5.1. Decentralization and Gender

Decentralization has influence on several socio-economic factors such as gender relations or equality between men and women. Women in the Ethiopian society are marginalized and have limited access to resources, services and power mainly due to cultural and religious factors. As a result they are disproportionately affected by poverty and suffer from violations of their human rights (Yigremew, Nega and Haregewoin 2005).

An earlier wereda study conducted by the World Bank (2001) found women's participation in community planning and decision making to be non-existent. Social factors were thought to have militated against women's presence and/or participation in planning and decision making. These include women's perception of themselves as disadvantaged in public speaking, workload, fear of reprisals by husbands if they speak at public fora, etc. Cultural factors were also found to have interfered with women's access to certain services. In this regard access to primary school and family planning are curtailed by cultural factors and men's hostility, respectively (World Bank 2001). This is an indication of the lack of women's voice in their local community and decentralization has had little impact on the situation.

There could be several ways of looking at evidence of the influence of decentralization on women. One way is to look at whether decentralization has facilitated legislation, policies and institutions that address the needs of women. Zenebework's (2001) observation in this regard is that in line with the process of decentralization, region's have established Women's Affairs Offices (WAB) and focal points in zones and the importance of women policy has also been stressed by states. Despite these, regional, zonal and wereda plans do not reflect the policies and strategies and there is no formal link between WABs and sector offices. In terms of elections, women are noted to have participated but their numbers dwindle as one goes up the hierarchy of regional structures. Zenebework (2001) also observes that women's involvement in the representative bodies has not challenged any gender bias in the society or in the structures of governance. This implies that there is a need for a gender sensitive electoral process.

In a field work conducted in three weredas, namely, Delanta-Dawnt, Hirshana, Bolosso Sorre in 2005, Yigremew, Nega and Haregewoin (2005) examined whether decentralization has empowered women. Empowerment is understood to mean ownership of economic resources; entitlement to social services (education and health); accessing knowledge and information and being involved in leadership and decision-making. The study reports limited economic empowerment by women as they are involved in informal and marginal activities, limited health services in the study weredas, limited access to information, limited participation in political leadership[4] and community development. The study also mentions that though in some weredas such as Wadla-Delanta, efforts are being made to ease the workload of women and encourage their participation in the communities' socio-economic activities, capacity limitation and weak institutional (associational) and resource constraints hinder the participation of women.

Whatever achievements are made in improving access to services, they are derived mainly from the work of NGOs such as Oxfam, UNICEF, and BESSO, which are active in the study weredas. For instance, some change in the attitude of the community towards women's participation and increased girls' participation in school are the results of NGO activities. The

---

[4] In Delanta-Dawnt, however, 42% of the wereda councilors were women, while this is very small in other weredas such as Harishin in Somali (4.3%), Bolosso Sore (2%).

study concludes that decentralization has not significantly benefited women, and gender mainstreaming is required in the decentralization policy in order to benefit women (Yigremew, Nega and Haregewoin 2005).

The above scant studies have touched on some aspects of gender in relation to decentralization. However, a systematic study investigating improvements in women's access to services and women's involvement in decentralized structures and decision making is necessary.

5.2 . Decentralization and Non-State Actors

The broad definition of Non-State Actors (NSAs) includes formally registered non-governmental organizations, trade unions, and professional organizations and a wide variety of informal, often community based, associations (BC 2004).

Decentralization should not be confined to the public sector alone. It should transfer power, responsibility and resources to non-state actors as well. In situations where power has been transferred to the non-public sector, local institutions are enhanced and receive space for representation and integration with the local government (Tegegne and Kassahun 2004). The Ethiopian decentralization does not open much space for the role of civil society and there is a widespread perception, especially amongst critics of decentralization, that government permeates all aspects of organizational/ institutional life, and that civil society is weak (Muir *et al.* 2004). Despite this, non-sate actors are seen as key players in the democratic and development process of the country by many donors (BC 2004). The relation between decentralization and non-state actors could be viewed from two perspectives. First it is expected that decentralization may encourage the formation of civic organizations at the local and regional levels and bring new dynamics in state-civil society relations. Second, decentralization can be enriched and facilitated by the existence of a vibrant civil society at the sub-national level (Teketel 2001).

Teketel (2001) outlines the influence of decentralization on civil society as follows. First, regional states have the mandate to register and license those civil society organizations operating within their respective regions and regulate the activities of those operating in the regions. This is considered as an indication of initiating a new process of relations between the regional and local governments and civil society organizations. Most regional states have also formulated a GO-NGO guideline to rationalize procedures and coordination of activities. Second, the Ethiopian decentralization system has provided a renewed impetus for the proliferation of ethnic-based associations, both region-wide and localized. The latter was also emphasized by Tegegne and Kassahun (2004) who say that the 'ethnic-based federal arrangement has helped in the mushrooming and strengthening of development associations'. Third, decentralization has not led to a significant growth of formal and independent civic organizations at grassroots level except the hierarchically organized women's and youth associations and formal multi-purpose agricultural cooperatives. Fourth, decentralization has not resulted in the expansion of civic organizations in remote regions. Fifth, professional and business associations are rare below regional levels. Sixth, rights and advocacy oriented civic organizations hardly emerge from regions. The above observations point to the little opportunity provided by the decentralization process in strengthening or encouraging civil society in Ethiopia. The sector thus remains weak and underdeveloped and the potential of decentralization in creating a vibrant civil society in Ethiopia seems unrealized. In this regard, however, it is very important and crucial to investigate what the constraints of decentralization are towards civil society in Ethiopia and what could also be done to stimulate civil society within the decentralized structure. Cognizant of this shortcoming, the government has recently embarked on finding means and ways of bridging this gap through recourse to what came to be known as Civil Society Capacity Building Program (CSCBP) whose progress is expected to go along with that of the Public Sector Capacity Building Program (PSCAP), which has been underway for some time now. To what extent this program has helped in strengthening the civil society within a decentralized structure, however, merits further study.

6.   The Way Forward

In the foregoing, different studies undertaken at various times on decentralization in Ethiopia are reviewed. In general, the studies under review have mainly dwelt on pertinent issues and themes of decentralization. These are associated with the reform measures of the post-1991 years in general and developments that transpired prior to the introduction of the recent District-Level Decentralization Program. This section tries to highlight, albeit briefly, gaps that are identified and what needs to be undertaken in order to bridge them and bring to light new information and knowledge.

6.1. Legal/Constitutional Arrangements and Institutional Setting

Challenges, opportunities, and strengths and weaknesses pertaining to the legal and political arrangements and the institutional settings that are in place are not studied and critically analyzed. Principles and arrangements regarding these issues are too general and pronounced as declarations of intent at best. Whether what are presented as solemn pledges and declarations are feasible and expedient to be put into practice in the face of the diversities characterizing sub-national units of governance, which are the targets of the decentralization drive, is not yet subjected to scientific and empirical research and critical analysis. One area that suffers from paucity of adequate attention pertains to examining the ramifications of ethno-linguistic considerations as a cornerstone of decentralization and regional-local self-rule. These are mentioned briefly and in passing in the various studies that are focused on different themes of decentralization. Hence this could be one area of future research interest that is worth considering.

6.2 Fiscal decentralization

Most studies of fiscal decentralization as it pertains to federal-regional relations were conducted prior to the recent wereda-level decentralization. These studies emphasized expenditure distribution, revenue sources and assignments, and adequacy of revenue sources at federal and regional levels. The conclusion they have arrived at highlighted the presence of fiscal imbalance and the inadequacy of such measures as inter-governmental transfer and borrowing to deal with imbalances. The extent to which intergovernmental transfer has achieved the goals of equity and balanced regional development is not adequately treated. The studies also revealed that regions depend considerably on the federal government for overcoming deficits that they encounter. The reasons behind such a high degree of dependence are associated with inadequacy of revenue sources allotted to regions and poor administrative and technical capacity of regions to efficiently collect revenues and utilize them. Though some studies attributed the underlying cause of dependence to the former, there is a need to indicate which of these factors are prominent and thereby find possible solutions to the problem. The implications of dependence on grants for future regional development endeavors also need to be examined and assessed in view of the quest to consolidate the federal system. The above being some of the possible areas for further reflection and investigation, there is limited recent and up-to-date literature on fiscal decentralization in Ethiopia. One research issue that is worth considering in this regard could be examining aspects of change and continuity pertaining to fiscal decentralization in Ethiopia. Knowledge gap on this issue has impeded efforts towards obtaining reliable and conclusive information. Future studies should, therefore, focus on examining recent trends and compare the situation with those of the past by discerning the factors that are responsible for similarities and/or differences (as the case may be).

Since the commencement of wereda decentralization, regions have started to transfer subsidies to local governments to enable the latter deliver service efficiently. The established federal formula and the unit-cost approach are the two ways of allocating resources from regions to weredas. Though some regions claim that the unit-cost approach is effective in enabling weredas to allocate budget for service delivery, there is no systematic study on the rationale and the impact of unit-cost approach as distinct from the formula in allocating resources. The block grant scheme is not the only way of transferring resources. Budget adjustment, contingency assistance, training support, food security grants and aid, and asset transfer are some of the different modalities used to transfer resources from regions to local governments. The merits of these different instruments, including the block grant system, have not been fully established. In other words, there is a need to evaluate the block and non-block grant or the unconditional and conditional systems of resource transfers from different perspectives. The revenue raising capacities of weredas vary significantly. Remote weredas compared to peri-urban weredas have a lower revenue collection and raising capacity. A study on these differences could be useful to identify any institutional gap that may be constraining to some weredas.

6.3 Wereda Decentralization - DLDP

It is now about four years since the DLDP commenced. In spite of the fact that this is relatively brief in terms of duration, the value added of DLDP in view of increased autonomy, adequacy of resource flows, poverty reduction and employment creation, and augmented capacity and revenue sources, among others, is not sufficiently studied and articulated in a rigorous manner. It could be argued that a time span of four years would allow one to modestly discern patterns and trends on whether there is the likelihood of realizing tangible outcomes accruing from the policy measure. Aspects of change and continuity (e.g., past experiences like dependence on higher tiers) and areas that call for improvement through new policy interventions warrant further studies that could contribute to policy making endeavors.

6.4 Municipal Decentralization

One of the recent phenomena in the Ethiopian decentralization drive is municipal decentralization. Regions have now enacted legislations to empower municipalities. The Amhara, Oromia, Tigray, and SNNP Regions are the main players in this regard. Reform towns have been identified and their numbers have increased from time to time. While this is a welcome step, there is no endeavor to study the impacts of such reforms and whether the reforms have really brought about differences in the various operations of municipalities, namely, service delivery, economic development, etc. Moreover, whether the reform has really empowered municipalities in enhancing their autonomy and resource generation capacity remains unknown. In addition, as municipal activities are currently classified as municipal and state functions and since it is only recently that some regions are contemplating on integrating the two, there is a need to assess whether integration would advance municipal development or not.

6.5 Decentralization and Service Delivery

Research on issues such as accountability of service providers to users, representation and participation of users in planning and decision making processes, and structures for participation and representation is almost lacking. What is often mentioned in the various studies undertaken to date relate to guided involvement of communities and service users in committees (PTAs/KETBs, health and environmental protection groups, etc.). In the light of this, there is a need to examine the state of affairs with regard to the role of CBOs, CSOs, and other formal and informal community organizations in articulating community priorities and preferences, and the prospects for self-empowerment in the pursuit of priority goals.

6.6 Decentralization, Socio-economic Development and Poverty Reduction

Several sector strategies, including pro-poor policies have been issued by the Ethiopian Government with the declared aim of improving living standards. Some of these are in line with the decentralization drive while others are not. There is sufficient reason to believe that decentralization might have some impact on these policies either in facilitating or constraining their implementation. The extent to which there is synergy between them needs to be examined. Such studies are lacking from the literature and efforts along this line will be a welcome addition to the existing body of literature. Decentralization might have a role in improving access to infrastructure provision since responsibilities in this regard (roads, education and health) are devolved to local governments. While there is some evidence indicating improvement in access to such services, the impact of decentralization on the quality of the services is not yet clearly known. In fact some studies have asserted that infrastructural quality has deteriorated and this needs to be well documented as a basis for embarking on alternative courses of action.

The decentralization-poverty reduction link in Ethiopia is a very important issue. Not only is decentralization considered as one instrument for expediting the poverty reduction strategies of the country. It could also be argued that decentralization provides the setting for the poor for increased participation in local decision making and representation, which contributes towards reducing vulnerability and insecurity. Some studies that tried to examine the link between poverty reduction and decentralization are done prior to the introduction of the wereda-level decentralization program, and they heavily relied on desk studies that were supplemented with brief field visits. If decentralization is used as an instrument for poverty reduction and is believed to have a positive impact on such efforts, there is a need for systematic studies that could determine the possible links between the two and the impacts thereof.

6.7 Implementation of the Decentralization Policy

Though official statistics and activity reports on progress in decentralization abound, there is no clear information on what has been achieved owing to the introduction of the policy regarding performance in the various sectors. What is often reported as achievement is not clearly articulated as having been realized as a result of the decentralization policy or other policies and attendant practices. Hence there is a need to undertake periodic studies (mid-term reviews) that would examine progress made as a result of the introduction and implementation of the decentralization policy.

6.8 Decentralization, Environment, Gender and Non-state Actors

A decentralized structure is believed to have pervasive effects on various socio-economic structures. Environment, gender and non-state actors exhibit some relations with a decentralized structure. As regards issues surrounding the environment, a decentralized structure enables decentralized resource management thereby contributing towards improved environmental management. Studies undertaken on this issue in Ethiopia to date have failed to specify whether the goals of decentralization correlate with the goals of resource management. How resource management has benefited from decentralization and what needs to be improved if resource management is to benefit from a decentralized structure needs to be clearly articulated. Though lack of capacity, authority, and resources were cited as constraints, there is a need to clearly establish the impacts of these shortcomings and assess their magnitude.

A decentralized structure is expected to change women's role by enhancing access to services, decision making, and empowerment at the local level. The few studies that dealt with gender and decentralization have concluded that though there are institutions pertinent to women's affairs, there is still a need for more gender sensitive policies, plans and programs. The studies have also claimed that the existing decentralized structures have not benefited women from the point of view of empowering and providing them with access to decision making. According to the studies, some improvements in the role of women in Ethiopia are believed to be due to NGO activities rather than decentralization. While this observation may be true, it is important to undertake comparative studies on the role of women in localities where NGO operations are underway and otherwise. Further, it is important to study how women fare in local politics and identify factors that explain the prevalent state of affairs.

A study on civil society and decentralization in Ethiopia has indicated that decentralization has played a limited role in creating a vibrant civil society. While this is an important finding, it is crucial to identify the constraints of decentralization in this regard. In addition, civil society is also expected to influence the pace and progress of decentralization in the country. One issue of research interest in this respect could be to examine to what extent and in what ways the existing civil society organizations have influenced decentralization.

Bibliography

Aalen, Lovise. 2002. *Ethnic federalism in a dominant party state: The Ethiopian experience 1991-2000*. Bergen: Chr. Michelsen Institute. Report R2002:2.

Abebe Jaleta. 2000. The impact of decentralization on access to and equity of education in Ethiopia: A case study of Adama and Fentale Weredas, East Shoa Zone. MA Thesis, Regional and Local Development Studies, Addis Ababa University.

AHE Consultants. 2005. Assessment of district level decentralization and capacity building progress in Amhara Regional State. DfID Study Report, Addis Ababa.

_____. 2005. Assessment of district level decentralization and capacity building progress in Tigray Regional State. DfID Study Report, Addis Ababa.

Amhara National Regional State (ANRS). 2003. Proclamation no. 91/2003: The Revised proclamation for the establishment, organization and definition of powers and duties of urban centers of the Amhara National Region, Bahir Dar.

Befekadu Degefe. 1994. The legal framework for fiscal decentralization in Ethiopia. In *Fiscal decentralization in Ethiopia*, edited by Eshetu Chole. Addis Ababa: Addis Ababa University Press.

Bereket Tassew. 2000. Aspect of decentralization practice in Sidama Zone. MA Thesis, AAU, Addis Ababa.

British Council (BC). 2004. Mapping non-state actors in Ethiopia: A research study commissioned by the European Union and the Ministry of Capacity Building, Ethiopia.

Canadian International Development Agency (CIDA). 2005. Ethiopia: Grassroots empowerment: Review of progress and prospects. Phase I, PLAN-NET Ltd., Calgary.

Chris, Heymans,, and Mohammed Musa. 2004. The Ethiopian IGR: Intergovernmental fiscal reforms in Ethiopia, trends and issues. World Bank. Addis Abeba

Cohen, John M. 1997. Decentralization and 'ethnic federalism' in post-civil war Ethiopia. In *Rebuilding societies after the civil war: Critical role for international assistance*, edited by Krishna Kumar. Boulder: Lynne Rienner.

Cohen, J. M., and Peterson S. B. 1994. Opening Pandora's Box: Preliminary notes on fiscal decentralization in contemporary Ethiopia. *Northeast African Studies*, 1 (1).

Degarge Minale, Befekadu, Zeleke and Wossenu Yimam. 2000. Decentralization and environmental protection in Ethiopia: Implications for sustainable development. A research report submitted to Organization for Social Science Research in Eastern and Southern Africa. Addis Ababa: OSSREA.

De Jong, Karign, Christiane Loquai and Iina Soiri, eds. 1999. Regionalizing poverty? In *Decentralization and poverty reduction: Exploring the linkages,* edited by Karjin de Jong, Christiane Loquai and Iina Soiri. Helsinki: Institute of Development Studies, University of Helinski, and European Centre for Development Policy Management (ECDPM).

Dereje Getahun. 2000. Urban service delivery: A case study of Bahir Bar with particular emphasis on solid waste management. MA Thesis, Addis Ababa University, Addis Ababa.

Dom, C., and Mohammed Musa. 2006. Review of implementation of the decentralization policy: A sample survey in six weredas of Amhara region. (Draft) Report prepared for the Embassy of Sweden and ANRS. Addis Ababa.

_____. 2006. Review of implementation of the decentralization policy: A sample survey in four sentinel weredas of Tigray Region. A report submitted to the Embassy of Ireland in Ethiopia and the Regional Government of Tigray. Addis Ababa.

_____. 2006. Briefing paper on review of "Implementation of the decentralization policy: A sample survey in four sentinel weredas of Tigray Region. Addis Ababa.

_____. 2006. Review of implementation of the decentralization policy: A sample survey in six weredas of Amhara Region. A report prepared for Embassy of Sweden, and Amhara National Regional State (ANRS). Addis Ababa.

Edegilign Hailu. 2006. An assessment of linkages between decentralization and poverty reduction with particular reference to pro-poor service delivery: The case of Yem special wereda. MA thesis, Department of Geography, Addis Ababa University.

Eshetu Chole. 1994. Issues of vertical imbalance in Ethiopia's emerging system of fiscal decentralisation. *Ethiopian Journal of Economics*, 3(2): 25-48.

Federal Democratic Republic of Ethiopia (FDRE). 1995. *The Constitution of the Federal Democratic Republic of Ethiopia*. Addis Ababa: FDRE.

Fenta Mandefro. 1998. Decentralization in post-Derg Ethiopia: Aspects of Federal-Regional relations. MA Thesis, Regional and Local Development Studies, Addis Ababa University.

Gebrehiwet Tesfai. 2002. Fiscal decentralization: The case of the government of national state of Tigrai. MA Thesis, Regional and Local Development Studies, Addis Ababa University.

Getachew Adem. 2001. Decentralization and economic development. Paper presented at the FSS symposium on "Decentralization and Development: Issues of Empowerment and Civil Society in Ethiopia", 26 October, Addis Ababa.

Gulyani, S. *et al.* 2001. Municipal decentralization in Ethiopia: A rapid assessment. Draft report. Addis Ababa.

Hamdok, A. 2003. Governance and policy in Africa: Recent experiences. In Reforming *Africa's institutions: Ownership, incentives, and capabilities*, edited by Kayizze-Mugerwa. New York: United Nations University Press.

Institute of Educational Research (IER). 2002. Ethiopia: Corruption survey. Addis Ababa University.

Jemal Abagissa. 2000. The financial management of Jimma town. MA Thesis, Regional and Local Development Studies, Addis Ababa University.

Joint Support Mission. 2005. Aide Memoire, Addis Ababa.

Jozsef, Hegedu, Mohammed Mussa and Peterson George. 2006. Review of regional-local government transfers in Ethiopia with special analysis and recommendation for the development of the Amhara Region's grant structure. The Urban Institute.

Jutting *et al*. 2004. Decentralization and poverty in developing countries: Exploring the impact. Working Paper No. 236. OECD Development Center.

Kassahun Berhanu and Tegegne Gebre-Egziabher. 2004. Citizen participation in the decentralization process in Ethiopia. A consultancy report submitted to the Ministry of Capacity Building, GoE, Addis Ababa.

Kibre Moges. 1994. The conceptual framework for fiscal decentralization. In *Fiscal decentralization in Ethiopia*, edited by edited by Eshetu Chole. Addis Ababa: Addis Ababa University Press.

Kumera Kenea. 2006. Decentralized governance and service delivery: A case study of Digelu and Tijo Wereda of Arsi Zone, Oromia Region. MA Thesis, Regional and Local Development Studies, Addis Ababa University.

Kurey, B., and Ruth Alsop. 2004. Empowerment in Ethiopia: A status review. Draft Working Paper. Addis Ababa

Larson, A.M. 2002. Natural resources and decentralization in Nicaragua: Are local governments up to the job? *World Development,* Vol. 30, no.1: 17-31.

Lissane Yohannes and Mohammed Mussa. 2005. Synthesis report on assessment of district level decentralization and capacity building progress in Tigray, Amhara, Oromia and SNNP regional states. Addis Ababa.

Lulseged Ageze. 2000. Fiscal decentralization and development in Ethiopia. Preliminary assessment presented at the symposium organized for reviewing Ethiopia's socio-economic performance (1991-1999). Inter-Africa Group, April, Addis Ababa.

Meheret Ayenew. 2002. Decentralization in Ethiopia: Two case studies on devolution of power and responsibilities to local government authorities. In *Ethiopia: The challenge of democracy from below,* edited by Bahru Zewde and Siegfreid Pausewang. Uppsala: Nordiska Afrikainstitutet; Addis Ababa: Forum for Social Studies.

_____. 2002. Decentralized municipal management in Ethiopia: A rapid appraisal of five municipalities. World Bank. Addis Ababa.

_____. 2001. Decentralization and democratic governance in Ethiopia: Lessons of experience and policy implications at the woreda level. Paper presented at the FSS symposium on "Decentralization and Development: Issues of Empowerment and Civil Society in Ethiopia", 26 October, Addis Ababa.

_____. 1998. Some preliminary observations on institutional and administrative gaps in Ethiopia's decentralization processes. Working Paper No. 1, September. Regional and Local Development Studies, Addis Ababa University.

Melkamu Bessie. 2004. Fiscal decentralization in Ethiopia: A review of problems of fiscal imbalance with reference to the case of Benishangul-Gumuz Region. MA Thesis, Addis Ababa University, Addis Ababa.

Minas Hiruy. 2003. Urban management and development in Ethiopia. In *The role of urbanization in the socio-economic development process*, edited by Berhanu Nega and Befekadu Degefe. Addis Ababa: Ethiopian Economic Policy Research Institute.

Ministry of Capacity Building (MCB). 2006. Local Government Policy Framework of the Federal Democratic Republic of Ethiopia, MoCB, March. Addis Ababa.

_____. 2005. "An Overview of District Level Decentralization and Capacity Building: A Report on the Assessment of Rural Woredas and Kebeles in Four Regional States. Addis Ababa.

_____. 2004. District Level Decentralization Program (DLDP): Action Plan 2005-2008. Addis Ababa.

Ministry of Finance and Economic Development (MoFED), GOE. 2005. Wereda-city benchmarking survey, Part II. Addis Ababa (Draft).

_____. 2002. Ethiopia: Sustainable Development and Poverty Reduction Program (SDPRP). Addis Ababa.

Ministry of Urban Works and Development (MWUD). 1999. Legal status, roles, responsibilities and relationships of municipalities in the Amhara National Regional State. Addis Ababa.

_____. 2006. Report and recommendation on municipal finance, SNNP Region. Addis Ababa.

Mohammed Abagojam. 1999. An Assessment of the current decentralized regional and local development experience in Oromia Region (1992-1996/97): Challenge and prospects. MA Thesis, AAU, Addis Ababa.

Mohammed Musa. 2005. Assessment of district level decentralization and capacity building progress in Oromia Regional State. DfID Study Report (Draft). Addis Ababa.

Mohammed Mussa. 2005. Assessment of district level decentralization and capacity building progresses in SNNP Regional State. Addis Ababa.

Mohammed Seiyd Yimer. 2006. The performance of wereda decentralization and empowerment program in Amhara Regional State: The case of Legambo Wereda. MA Thesis, Regional and Local Development Studies, Addis Ababa University.

Molla Megistu. 2004. An enquiry into the design of intergovernmental transfers and fiscal decentralisation in Ethiopia, Ph.D. Dissertation, Vienna University of Economics and Business Administration.

Muir, A. 2005. Action learning for improved service delivery and local governance (ALI), Ethiopia: Scoping exercise. Addis Ababa.

Muir *et al.* 2004. Building capacity in Ethiopia to strengthen the participation of citizens' associations in development: A study of the organizational associations of citizens. Paper prepared for the World Bank. Addis Ababa.

Mulualem Besse. 2001. Institutional and administrative capacity for development: The case of Benishangul-Gumuz Regional State: Efforts, problems and prospects. MA Thesis, Regional and Local Development Studies, Addis Ababa University.

Parry, T. R. 1997. *Achieving balance in decentralization: A case study of education in decentralization in Chile.* Athens, USA: University of Georgia Press.

Rondinelli, D. A. 1993. *Development projects as policy experiments: An adaptive approach to development administration.* London and New York: Routledge.

Tegegne Gebre-Egziabher. 2000. Regional development planning in Ethiopia: Past experiences, current initiatives and future prospects. *Eastern Africa Social Science Research Review (EASSRR),* vol. XI, no. 1: 65-92.

Tegegne Gebre-Egziabher, Assefa Admassie, Kassahun Berhanu, Meheret Ayenew. 2004. Monitoring the progress of governance in Africa: The case of Ethiopia. UNECA and RLDS, AAU, Addis Ababa.

Tegegne Gebre-Egziabher and Kassahun Berhanu. 2004. The role of decentralized governance in building local institutions, diffusing ethnic conflicts, and alleviating poverty in Ethiopia. *Regional Development Dialog,* Vol. 25, no. 1: 35-63.

Teketel Abebe. 2001. Decentralization and civil society. Paper presented at the FSS symposium on "Decentralization and Development: Issues of Empowerment and Civil Society in Ethiopia", 26 October, Addis Ababa. Addis Ababa.

Tesfaye Digie. 2000. The impact of decentralization on efficiency and meritocracy of the civil service in Ethiopia: The case of Oromiya and Southern Nations, Nationalities, and Peoples' Region (SNNPR). MA Thesis, Regional and Local Development Studies, Addis Ababa University.

Tesfaye Mergia. 2005. Tax Assignment to sub-national governments in a decentralized fiscal system of Ethiopia. MA Thesis, Addis Ababa University, Addis Ababa.

Transitional Government of Ethiopia (TGE). 1991. *The Transitional Period Charter.* Addis Ababa.

_____. 1992. Proclamation No. 7/1992 providing for the establishment of national/regional self-governments. Addis Ababa: FDRE.

_____. 1992. Proclamation No. 33/1992: A proclamation to define the sharing of revenue between the central government and the national/regional self-governments. Addis Ababa.

United Nations Capital Development Fund (UNCDF). 2003. *Local government initiative: Pro-poor infrastructure and service delivery in rural Sub-Sahara Africa.* New York: UNCDF.

Van der Loop, Theo, ed. 2002. *Local democracy and decentralization in Ethiopia.* Addis Ababa: Regional and Local Development Studies (RLDS) and UN-HABITAT.

Worku Yehualashet. 2004. District level decentralization in Ethiopia. Addis Ababa.

World Bank. 2002. Wereda studies. Vol. II, Annexes I-III. World Bank Country Office, Ethiopia. Addis Ababa.

_____. 2002. Municipal decentralisation in Ethiopia: A rapid assessment (revised) http:/www.worldbank.org/afr/et/reports/2001_gulyani.pdf.

_____. 2001. Ethiopia: Wereda study. Vol. I. World Bank Country Office, Addis Ababa.

_____. 2000. Regionalisation Study Report, No. 18898-ET. Addis Ababa.

_____. 1997. *The role of government in East Asian economic development: A comparative institutional analysis.* Oxford: Clarendon Press.

Yigremew Adal, Nega Wubie and Haregewoin Cherinet. 2005. *Study on the implementation of decentralization policy in Ethiopia.* Addis Ababa: Oxfam GB.

Zenebework Taddesse. 2001. Gender and decentralization. Paper presented at the FSS symposium on "Decentralization and Development: Issues of Empowerment and Civil Society in Ethiopia", 26 October, Addis Ababa.

Annex 1: Expenditure Assignment in Ethiopia

Central Government	Regional Government
• Defense,	• All matters with the exception of those listed in column 1,
• Foreign affairs,	• Borrow from domestic lending sources and levy duties and taxes,
• Economic policy,	• Issue and implement laws and rules relating to public services which do not conflict with the relevant policy of the central government,
• Conferring of citizenship,	
• Declaration of state of emergency,	
• Deployment of army where situations beyond the capacity of regional government arise,	• Establish, direct and supervise social and economic development establishments or enterprises,
• Printing of currency,	• Prepare, approve, and implement their own budgets,
• Establishing and administering major development establishment,	• Administer, develop and protect their natural resources,
• Building and administering major communications networks and the like,	• Employ and administer their own personnel in accordance with the public service and pension laws of the central

government,

- Establish and direct security and policy forces in accordance with the policy and directives of the central government,

- Establish judicial organs to decide on matters not specifically assigned to the central government,

- Own properties of the region, acquire ownership of property and transfer property.

Annex 2: Revenue Assignment in Ethiopia

Central Government	Regional Government	Central and Regional Government
• Duties, taxes and other charges levied on the importation and exportation of goods;	• Personal income tax collected from employees of the regional governments and employees other than those covered under sub article 2 and 4 of this Article	• Profit tax, personal income tax and sales tax collected from enterprises jointly owned by the central government and regional government;
• Personal income tax collected from employees of the central Government and international organizations;	• Rural land use fee	• profit tax, dividend tax and sales tax collected from organizations;
• Profit tax, personal income tax and sales tax collected from enterprises owned by the Central Government	• agricultural income tax collected from farmers not incorporated in an organization	• profit tax, royalty (*sic*) and rent of land collection from large scale mining, any petroleum and gas operations
• Taxes collected from national lotteries and other chances wining prizes;	• profits and sales tax collected from individual traders;	
• taxes collected on income from air, train and marine transport activities;	• tax on income from inland water transportation;	
	• tax collected from rent of	

• Taxes collected from rent of houses and properties owned by the Central Government • Charges and fees on licenses and services issued or rendered by the Central Government	house and properties owned by the Regional Government • profit tax, personal income tax and sales tax collected from enterprises owned by the Regional Governments; • without prejudice to sub-article 4(c) of this Article, income tax, royalty (sic) and rent of land collected from mining activities; • charges and fees on licenses and services issued or rendered by the Regional Government

Annex 3: Road Network Development in Ethiopia (1997-2005)

Year	Asphalt (km)	Gravel (km)	Rural (km)	Total (km)	Growth rate	Road density/1000 population	Road density/1000 sq km
1997	3708	12162	10680	26550		0.46	24.14
1998	3760	12240	11737	27237	4.5	0.46	25.22
1999	3812	12250	12600	28662	3.3	0.47	26.06
2000	3824	12250	15480	31554	10.1	0.50	28.69
2001	3924	12467	16480	32871	4.2	0.50	29.88
2002	4053	12564	16680	33297	1.3	0.49	30.27
2003	4362	12340	17154	33856	1.7	0.49	30.78
2004	4635	13905	17956	36496	7.8	0.51	33.18
2005	4972	13640	18406	37018	1.4	0.51	33.60

Source: *Ethiopia Roads Authority 2006.*

II

A Rapid Assessment of Wereda Decentralization in Ethiopia

*Meheret Ayenew**

1. Background and Rationale

In 2002/2003, the Government of Ethiopia (GoE) launched the expanded program of wereda decentralization, otherwise known as District-Level Decentralization Program (DLDP), to deepen the process of decentralization down to Wereda level. The major thrust of the initiative was to devolve decision making authority to Weredas and transform them into strong institutions of local democratic governance and efficient means for delivering public services. The Government's intent was to gradually devolve power and resources to an estimated 550 Weredas[1] throughout the country, and this was considered a major governance reform agenda with considerable promises as well as challenges.

The Wereda decentralization policy was initially launched in 430 Weredas covering the four major regions of Amhara, Oromia, Tigray and Southern Nations, Nationalities and Peoples Regional State (SNNPRS), but was subsequently to be implemented in the other regions as well. Following the implementation of the Wereda Decentralization program, there has been some progress in enhancing the administrative and budgetary capacity of Wereda administrations with a view to creating local governance institutions with a greater degree of accountability and responsiveness to the needs and concerns of the community at the grassroots level (Lissane and Mohammed 2005; CIDA 2005). Despite the successes, however, there have been challenges in instituting viable Wereda administrations with the requisite capacity for self-government and local economic development. Some preliminary assessments indicate that most of the constraints that Wereda governments face emanate from inter-related factors, including poor and inadequate revenue base to undertake meaningful local economic development; shortage of competent staff

---

* Meheret Ayenew, Ph.D, Faculty of Business and Economics, Addis Ababa University.
[1] The precise number of Weredas ranges between 530-550 depending upon sources referred.

skilled in public services delivery; lack of experience in decentralized governance; and the absence of an effective legal and policy framework for Wereda decentralization (Asmelash 1987; Meheret 1998; Fenta 1999).

The Wereda Decentralization Program was touted as a major step in empowering Wereda populations to participate in economic and political decisions affecting their lives. It was also presented as a major program to test the commitment of the Government to decentralized governance that will be more accountable to the people than to federal and regional government authorities. In many countries, embarking upon a major program of decentralization to empower the local people to determine their political and economic choices and administer matters in their jurisdiction has been an attractive political agenda, but its concrete realization has most often been illusive at worst and challenging at best. The Ethiopian experience in Wereda decentralization cannot be totally divorced from this observation.

There is broad consensus that devolving power and authority to Weredas is key to local empowerment and meaningful self-government. However, the full impact of the government's Wereda decentralization program and the challenges faced in instituting democratic governance structures have not been properly assessed. It is against this background that the Forum for Social Studies (FSS), with financial backing from the Norwegian Government, undertook a rapid assessment of the current status of Wereda decentralization. The major objective of the project is to assess the progress in devolving power and resources to Wereda Administrations, and identify gaps that will require further research and policy action by the Government of Ethiopia.

2. Organization of the Report

This report has 8 sections. Section 1 explains the rationale and background for the study. Sections 2 outlines the organization of the report and the main objectives of the study respectively. The approach and methodology of the study are discussed in Section 3. Section 4 presents a brief historical review of decentralization in Ethiopia. A theoretical discussion on decentralization is presented in Section 5 to provide a proper conceptual framework for assessing the current state of Wereda-level decentralization. Section 6 provides a brief historical overview of decentralization in Ethiopia. Section 7 presents an analysis of the field data and observations based on focus group discussions and interviews with Wereda executive committee members, councilors and members of the caretaker Kifle Ketema administrations in Addis Ababa City Government. A brief overview of budget administration in Wereda governments is provided in Section 8.

Preliminary findings that came out of the study are discussed in Section 9. Section 10 contains the conclusion part of the study.

3. Objectives of the Study

The overall objective of this research project is to conduct a rapid assessment of the degree of institutionalization of Wereda autonomy and capacity for local economic development since the launching of the decentralization policy in 2002/03. Specifically, the study aims to achieve the following:

- Assess the level of autonomy and decision making competence of Wereda governments;
- Appraise the administrative and institutional capacities of Weredas for local self-government and the provision of socio-economic services;
- Assess the budget and revenue capacity of Weredas to carry out development;
- Examine important aspects of inter-governmental relations, i.e., Wereda-region, -zone and -kebele relations;
- Provide preliminary data that will serve as a basis for preparing a proposal for an in-depth research on Wereda governance covering a large number of Weredas.

4. Approach and Methodology

Primary and secondary sources of information were employed to conduct a rapid assessment of the state of local governance at the Wereda level. A two-person research team consisting of Dr Meheret Ayenew (lead researcher) and Ato Aragaw Yimer (assistant researcher) carried out field work between 1st May 2006 – 30th June 2006 in 8 randomly selected Weredas from the 4 regions of Amhara, Oromia, SNNP and Tigray Regions. The sampled Weredas were selected in consultation with the respective heads of capacity building bureaus of the respective regions. In addition, two Kifle Ketemas—Arada and Addis Ketema Kifle Ketemas— were also randomly selected from Addis Ababa City Government for the rapid assessment exercise.

While carrying out the field work, the researchers used a semi-structured data sheet to collect background information. This included information pertaining to the socio-economic and demographic profile of the Weredas, their current governance and administration structure and the budget and financial capacities of each sampled Wereda. In addition, focus group discussions were held with Wereda administrators and councilors to assess the degree of institutionalization of Wereda-level decentralization and discuss the major challenges faced since the program was launched in 2002/2003.

The field work in the 8 Weredas and 2 Kifle Ketemas was conducted under time and budget constraints; that was why the rapid assessment approach focusing on key aspects of local governance and economic development was used. As a result of the short time duration for the project and the limited funds made available, Weredas which were easily accessible and on which limited research has been done in the past were purposively sampled for this study. Notwithstanding the constraints, however, the research team made intensive efforts to gather sufficient data and draw conclusions that will serve as a basis for developing appropriate, acceptable and effective policy recommendations for reforming local governance. As earlier pointed out, 2 Kifle Ketemas from Addis Ababa City Administration were also randomly selected for the field study to gain an insight into the level of autonomy and decision-making authority in an urban milieu.

While conducting the field work, the research team met and held discussions with Wereda administrators and members of the executive committee (i.e., cabinet) on the institutionalization of Wereda decentralization and the challenges faced in transforming Weredas into democratic structures for local self-rule and economic development. In addition, a semi-structured data check list was used to collect secondary data on the socio-economic and demographic profile of the Weredas; distribution and coverage of social services; governance/institutional and human resource capacities; and the fiscal and revenue strength of Wereda governments for providing services and undertaking local economic development. Such data provided a basis for drawing comparisons on the state of basic public services, such as access to education, health and clean water; and the state of institutional and administrative capacity for meaningful self-government among the 8 sampled Weredas.

The research team wishes to acknowledge the cooperation of many Wereda officials in providing data and sharing their experiences. The majority of the Weredas visited provided well-organized and informative socio-economic reports out of which valuable data were extracted for the study. A few Weredas lacked the administrative capacity, personnel skilled in report writing and compiling basic data, and essential office equipment, such as computers and photocopy machines, and only provided hand-written accounts of the socio-economic situation of their respective Weredas. Nevertheless, the reports provided by the Wereda administrations proved valuable in the writing of this research report. Generally, the more remote the Wereda and the more inaccessible it is, the more the dire shortage of trained staff and the less the chances for the Wereda to be endowed with such essential office equipment and trained personnel.

In this study, only a small fraction of the total number of Wereda tiers of government were sampled for field work. Hence, the conclusions and observations drawn on the basis of this limited field investigation must be considered as tentative and not be taken as generalizations applicable to all the Weredas throughout the country. What is needed is a more comprehensive and extensive study covering a large number of Wereda administrations that can yield important propositions and practical policy inputs for reforming the institutional structures and processes of Wereda governance, enhancing public services delivery and undertaking local socio-economic development.

5. Decentralization in Ethiopia: A Brief Historical Overview

Contemporary Ethiopia has limited experience in decentralized governance and administration. Throughout much of its recent history, the modern Ethiopian state has been a highly centralized polity leaving very little responsibility and authority to sub-national levels of administration. Ever since the beginnings of a modern public administrative system at the turn of the century, outlying governance and political sub-divisions of the country have most often operated by being subordinated to the formal authority of the central government. As a result, there evolved a deconcentrated administrative and governance system whereby local governments and branch offices of central government departments operated as field agents rather than as autonomous local government structures with full and adequate decision-making authority and control over resources. This kind of governmental structure hardly lends itself to democratic politics and participatory development at the local level. As a result, the tradition of a centralized and unitary state has persisted for a long period countervailing the evolution of a participatory and decentralized governance structure.

The foundation for a modern local government system was laid by Emperor Haile Selassie I more than half a century ago. The Imperial regime reorganized provincial administration by creating a four-tier local government structure that included *teklay gizat, awraja*, Wereda and *Mekitil* Wereda levels of administration[2]. The first comprehensive administrative decree No. 1 of 1942 defined the power and role of the Ministry of Interior as the principal central government department to supervise local government throughout the country. Governor generals (*Enderasses*) for

---

[2] Mikitil Weredas were later dropped and the country adopted a three-tier governmental system in the late 1950s.

teklay gizats and governors for *awraja* and Wereda governments were appointed by the central government to act as the representatives of the imperial throne in the periphery. The system was very much centralized because local government units had no authority over their budgets and could not undertake development on their initiative. It was also undemocratic because there were no elected local government councils or any other representative bodies to involve the people in governance and development at the different sub-national levels of administration (Clapham 1969; Meheret 1998).

The local government administrative structure put in place by the Imperial regime was intended to centralize power and resources in a strong central state leaving very little autonomy to the provinces. Most central ministries operated in the provinces through branch offices which had little or no decision-making authority at the local level. In practice, heads of such field offices were made to report to parent ministries as well as to provincial and awraja governors, who acted as representatives of the Ministry of Interior. This structural set up generated dual accountability in central-local relations that often created conflicts of authority and communication problems (Koehn 1974).

Following the collapse of imperial rule, the Derg government assumed power in 1974. But, it too did not have a better record at decentralizing power from the center to the periphery. The regime continued with the same tradition of a highly centralized post-imperial state inherited from its monarchist predecessor. It reinforced the tradition of a centralized state by instituting a Marxist-Leninist ruling party that imposed tight control on state and society. A radical land reform policy that nationalized rural and urban land was implemented thus ending many years of landed oligarchy. This was followed by sweeping nationalization of private businesses, including small and big factories, banks, insurance companies, etc., that helped to curve an all pervasive role for the state in the economy. Simply put, economic management and planning were state dominated and the government kept a tight rein on agriculture and rural development through the policy of state farms and state-imposed co-operativization of peasant agriculture (Dessalegn 1984; Clapham 1988; Andargatchew 1993).

The Derg was the most repressive regime that the country has seen in recent memory. The regime's repression had no bounds: thousands were arbitrarily killed, imprisoned and forced to flee the country. Its authoritarian rule generated ethnic-based opposition that resulted in fratricidal civil wars for nearly two decades (1974-991). The country was plunged in political turmoil and endless instability thanks to the regime's persistence to resolve political differences with the use of force rather than negotiations and compromises with the different protagonists that had different visions for the future of the Ethiopian state (Dessalegn and Meheret 2005).

One of the causes of resistance to the Derg was its highly centralist policies. The regime's uncompromising stance on a centralized polity generated a great deal of opposition by ethnic-based liberation movements who took up arms demanding secession and/or ethnic autonomy, particularly in the northern and south-eastern parts of the country. Tigray, Eritrea[3] and the Ogaden regions were the worst affected by unrest and ethnic-based liberation organizations that put up stiff resistance against the Derg. In the mid-1980's, the Derg issued a policy to grant limited administrative and political autonomy to quell the ethnic insurgency that bedeviled the three war-ravaged provinces—Eritrea, Tigray and the Ogaden. Given the Derg's track record of authoritarianism, the disaffected groups did not take this initiative as a genuine move to devolve state power and resources. The ethnic-based anti-Derg groups rejected the decentralization gesture outright because they considered it only a temporary respite to appease the widespread ethnic-based opposition. Simply put, it was viewed as a desperate attempt to buy time rather than as a genuine move to resolve the country's intractable ethnic problems. With the failure of the half-hearted decentralization reform effort under the most authoritarian regime, the country was thrown into further turmoil that precipitated the collapse of the regime and its replacement by the Ethiopian Peoples Revolutionary Democratic Forces (EPRDF) in May 1991 (Fukui and Markakis 1994; Meheret 1998).

When the EPRDF government came to power in 1991, it committed itself to a broad-based power structure and a decentralized state. Starting in 1995, it put in place a decentralization policy that aimed to transfer powers, responsibilities and resources from the central government to regional, zonal, Wereda and kebele levels of administration. On the surface, the step marked a radical departure from the country's hitherto long historical legacy of centralized political and governance. In reality, however, the concrete realization of genuine decentralization and democratic governance still remain unfulfilled promises. As indicated elsewhere in this report, limited experience in decentralized governance, undeveloped transport and communication infrastructure, and inadequate organizational and human resource capacity for democratic self-rule remain strong challenges militating against the institutionalization of decentralized and participatory governance in this country (Asmelash 2000; Meheret 1998).

---

[3] At the time, Eritrea was Ethiopia's northern most province, which later became a separate state in 1991 following a U.N. supervised referendum endorsed by the Ethiopian Government.

The 1995 Federal Constitution of the Government of Ethiopia (GoE) has formally created a federal state comprising regional sub-governments curved out on the basis of ethno-linguistic criteria. The federation comprises nine ethnic-based regional states and two autonomous administrations that include Tigray; Afar; Amhara; Oromia; Somali; Southern Nations, Nationalities, and Peoples Region (SNNPR); Benishangul-Gumuz; Gambella and Harrari national regional states; and Addis Ababa and Dire Dawa autonomous administrative areas. All the regional governments have been given substantial formal powers to plan and execute social and economic programs in their localities. The organization of regional governments follows the same pattern as the central government with elected assemblies that make laws and policies, a judicial branch of government and an executive administration that is responsible for the day-to-day running of the region. As per the 1995 federal constitution, regional governments enjoy a considerable degree of self-rule, including a constitution, a regional flag, the authority to prepare and administer budgets and the right to use regional languages of their choice in the courts, schools and public administration (TGE 1992; FDRE 1995).

At present, there are five levels of government in the Ethiopian federal structure, viz. the federal, regional, zonal, Wereda and kebele levels of government[4]. State functions have been formally divided between the federal and regional governments whereby the central government is responsible for national issues of concern, such as defence and national security, currency and foreign affairs, while regions are responsible for drawing and implementing budgets; providing public services such as primary and secondary education and health; carrying out socio-economic and infrastructure development at regional and local levels. Both the federal and regional constitutions provide for decentralized governance structures that guarantee periodic elections and popularly elected councils at all levels of administration. In sum, the formal division of powers envisage highly decentralized governmental structures whereby the central government has effectively transferred political and economic decision making authority to regional, zonal, wereda and kebele levels of government. The 5-tier structure of the organization of the Federal Ethiopian Government is presented in the following Figure I.

---

[4] Zonal administrations are formally recognized as tiers of government having elected councils and legally defined powers and authorities only in SNNPR. In other regions, zones are coordinating and supervisory administrative structures with no executive or policy making authority.

Fig I: Organizational Structure of the Five Levels of Government of the Federal Democratic Republic of Ethiopia

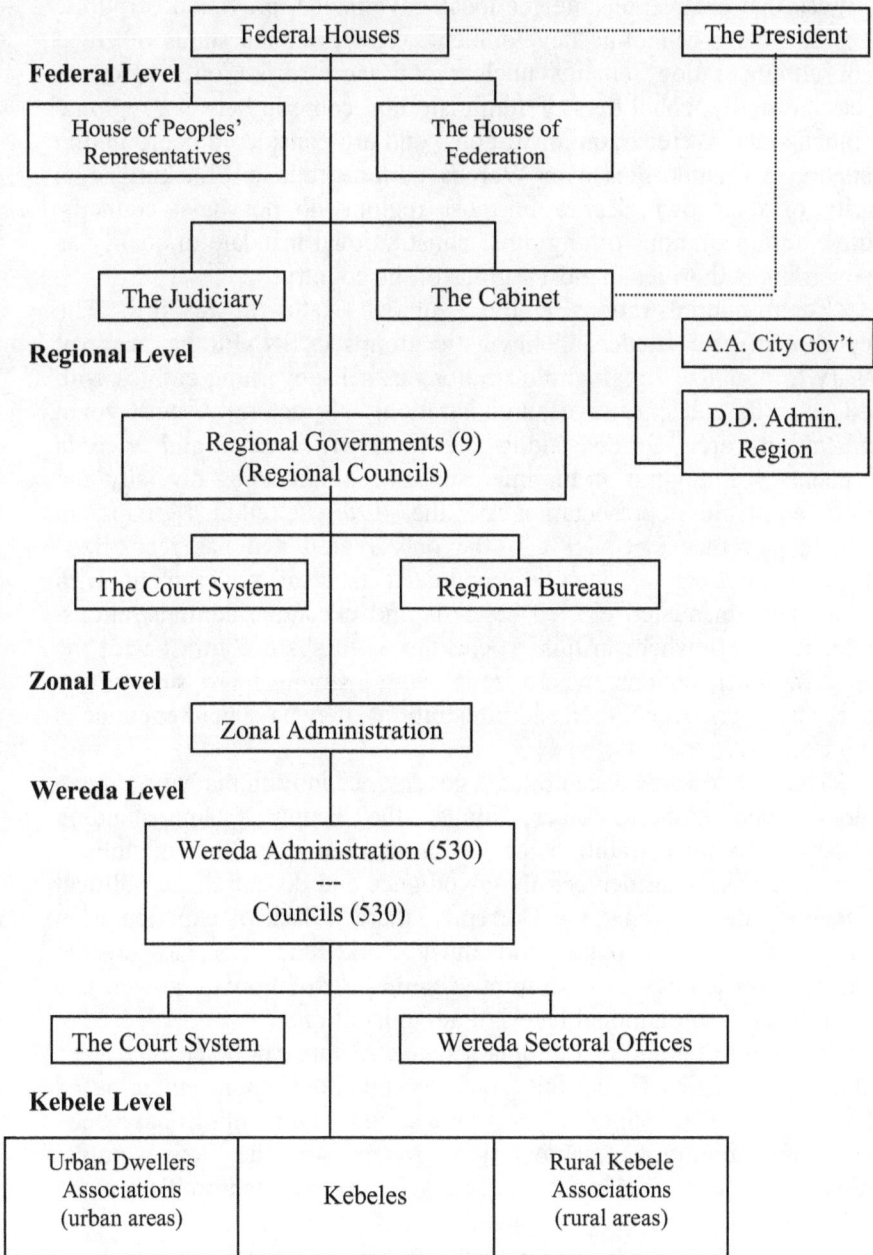

Source: Meheret 2002; CSA 2004; Field data 2006.

Within the framework of current state structure, Weredas and kebeles are constitutionally recognized tiers of local government. By law, these two levels of government have elected councils and executive committees that are responsible for local governance, provision of public services and socio-economic development. However, the status of zonal tiers of administration remains unclear and varies from one region to another. Formally, zonal tiers of administration come in between regional governments and Wereda administrations, and are considered coordinating and supervisory authorities over Wereda administrations. Lacking legal authority of their own, Zones in most regions do not have councils, executive administrations or any other constitutional mandate to qualify as self-governing authorities in most regions of the country.

Zonal administrations enjoy a unique status in SNNPR. The existence of diverse ethnic and linguistic groups in SNNPR has made it necessary to organize zonal administrations as self-governing entities with elected councils and executive administrations. Structurally, most zonal administrations are formed along the lines of regional and Wereda governments. Simply put, in the interests of accommodating diversity and ensuring equitable representation of the different ethnic groups in democratic governance, SNNPR is the only region that has recognized zonal administrations as legally recognized tiers of government with constitutionally mandated elected councils and executive administrations. As pointed out elsewhere in this article, this is in sharp contrast with the situation in other regions, where zonal administrations are supervisory administrative tiers over Wereda administrations; they have neither councils nor any executive authority.

The path towards decentralized governance in Ethiopia has not been a smooth ride. Among other things, the country's long-standing authoritarian political tradition has created seemingly insurmountable challenges in promoting democratic governance and decentralized political and economic decision-making. Currently, there is lack of experience on how a federal system ought and must work; and this has created considerable difficulties in instituting genuine devolution of power and responsibilities to sub-national levels of administration.

The current brand of Ethiopia's state structure can be characterized as ethnic federalism. Since the country embarked upon ethnic-based institutional federalism some 15 years ago, serious shortcomings have been observed in promoting democratic governance and active public participation in the development process. A frequently cited problem is the excessive concentration of governmental power and authority at regional government levels, which has rendered many Weredas dependent on regions for matters that are of largely local jurisdiction. An additional challenge to bring about effective devolution of responsibilities has been the limited administrative and resource capacity of Wereda governments. Many Wereda administrations are poorly staffed and under-financed to carry out the functions and responsibilities bestowed upon them, including managing the administration of their areas, providing public services, conducting democratic governance, administering law and order, running the school and education system and undertaking local economic and infrastructure development.

Based on the preceding discussion, it can be inferred that the policy of Wereda decentralization has not fully achieved its target of democratic governance and participatory development. Insufficient administrative and institutional capacity such as lack of well-trained local government personnel; top-down decision and authority structures afflicting the state system; absence of transparency and accountability at the local level; limited political space for non-state actors and non-ruling party organizations to partake in governance and development; and shortage of budgetary and financial resources frequently faced by Wereda governments are often cited as major limitations for promoting effective decentralization. These problems are more acute in some regions than in others reflecting both inter and intra-regional disparities in organizational and resource capacities. In addition, the degree of heterogeneity that exists among regions is also an important contributory factor to differences in institutional capabilities and resources for self-governance and local economic development.

6. Theoretical Discussion

Conceptually, decentralization as a generic term refers to the territorial distribution of power and functions between a sovereign state and its constituent parts, which can be regions, states or provinces. It denotes the dispersal of power and authority through the geographical hierarchy of the state and the institutions and processes through which such dispersal occurs. It entails the subdivision of the state's territory into smaller areas and the creation of political and administrative institutions for self-rule and democratic participation by the communities in those areas. In essence, these administrative and political sub-divisions are self-governing entities that enjoy independent decision-making power and exercise a considerable degree of autonomy in defined jurisdictions (Smith 1985; Slater 1989).

In assessing the impact of official decentralization policies on democratic governance, it is necessary to make a distinction between two important concepts in decentralization, viz. Devolution (political decentralization) and deconcentration (administrative decentralization). These two patterns of decentralization have different goals and purposes. It is necessary to discuss some important differences between the two approaches in order to provide a framework for assessing whether or not decentralization has helped in transferring adequate decision making authority and resources to Wereda governments since the GoE launched the current program in 2002/2003.

The essence of deconcentration or administrative decentralization is intra-government transfer of authority and functions among units of administration in the same governmental structure. It represents an administrative arrangement whereby authority and responsibility flow from top to bottom in a single organizational hierarchy. Regional and local governments function as organizations of field administration rather than as independent decision making centers. In practice, deconcentration involves delegation of responsibilities by central headquarters to field administrations or branch offices within the same bureaucratic apparatus. An important feature of such an administrative arrangement is that decision-making authority is retained by a central bureaucracy and branch offices are only extensions to execute policies and plans formulated by central authorities. In other words, the discretion of local authorities and branch offices in matters of decision making is highly restricted because they do not have independent legal existence of their own (Rondinelli and Cheema 1983).

Devolution or political decentralization on the other hand is a governance arrangement aimed at achieving transfer of decision-making power and political responsibility to sub-national levels of government. Conceptually, devolution is a formal transfer of authority and responsibility to legally constituted local government authorities. This pattern of decentralization represents a system of political administration whereby authority and responsibility are constitutionally shared between the central government and other subsidiary units of governments, which can be states, regions, provinces or chartered municipalities. The primary objective of political decentralization is to push decision-making down to lower levels of governments and empower communities to exercise self-rule at the local level. In sum, this approach to decentralization has the single most important advantage of advancing democratic governance because it effectively transfers decision-making authority from the central government to local governance structures (Smith 1985; Manor 1985)

Devolution or political decentralization is usually assumed to entail democracy. As such, the following are its intended benefits:

- Transferring power and authority from the central government to legally established units of local government;

- Promoting democracy at the local level through periodic elections and elected councils;

- Encouraging citizen participation in government and development;

- Guaranteeing the institutional and fiscal autonomy of local government authorities;

- Guaranteeing the independent decision-making authority of local governments;

- Promoting accountability and responsiveness of administrations to the citizenry;

- Helping in the development of a robust civil society;

- Promoting equity at the local level by ensuring the fair representation of all societal groups in the community.

The goals of *political decentralization* enumerated above are often used as yardsticks to assess the success of decentralization policies in promoting democracy. If a decentralization program achieves most of these ideals, it can be characterized as successful in promoting democratic governance. By the same token, the Wereda decentralization policy can be said to have contributed to democracy in the country if it has promoted some of the ideals of political decentralization, including democratic self-rule; sufficient and broad political space for competitive politics at the local level; independent decision-making authority to Wereda governments; popular public participation in governance and development; democratic representation; empowerment and equity. In this study, these set of parameters of political decentralization will be used to critically assess the state of democratic governance and participatory development at Wereda levels of administration.

7. Data Presentation and Analysis

7.1 Socio-economic and Demographic Profile

The 8 Weredas that were randomly selected for conducting the rapid assessment of Wereda decentralization of the Government of Ethiopia (GoE) launched in 2002/2003 included Mecha and Dera; Mullo Sullulta and Yaya Gullele ; Alaba and Silti; and, Kilte Awlalo and Seharti-Samre from Amhara, Oromia, SNNPR and Tigray regions, respectively. All the Weredas have predominantly agricultural and largely subsistence rural economies with considerable differences in terms of the level of infrastructure development and coverage of and residents' access to social and economic services. The geographical distribution and population sizes

of the sampled Weredas and the 2 Kifle Ketemas in Addis Ababa City
Government are provided in table 1.

Table 1. Population of 8 sampled Weredas and 2 Kifle Ketemas, 2005/2006

No.	Name of Wereda/Kifle Ketema	Population		Total
		M	F	
1.	Mehca (Amhara)	168,784	166,746	335,530
2.	Dera (Amhara)	118,658	126,502	245,160
3.	Mullo Sullulta (Oromia)	67,956	72,738	140,694
4.	Yaya Gulele (Oromia)	---	---	75,646[5]
5.	Alaba (SNNPR)	115,103	110,200	225,303
6.	Silti (SNNPR)	99,632	103,699	203,331
7.	Kilte Awlalo (Tigray)	110,726	111,988	222,714
8.	Seharti-Samre (Tigray)	58,887	62,131	121,018
9.	Arada Kifle Ketema (Addis Ababa City Government)	169,988	182,672	352,660
10.	Addis Ketema Kifle Ketema (Addis Ababa City Government)	196,000	204,000	400,000

Source: Field data 2006.

As can be observed from table 1, all the Weredas except Yaya
Gulele in Oromia have populations greater than 100,000. Indeed, Alaba
and Silti in SNNPR, Mecha and Dera from Amhara region and Kilte
Awlalo from Tigray region have well over 200,000 inhabitants. In the
course of the discussion with Wereda administrators, there was widespread
feeling that government policy making, including the decentralization
program, was premised on the notion that a Wereda had an average
population ranging between 100,000-120,000. According to the discussants,
an issue of even greater importance was the fact that it was this figure
which was used as one of the sets of criteria in the allocation of budgets to
Wereda governments at the federal and regional levels. It can also be noted
from the table 1 that the 2 Kifle Ketemas, which are predominantly more
urban than Wereda governments, are more densely populated than any of
the Weredas in the 4 major regions. This may make it necessary to use
different methodologies and sampling techniques to conduct an in-depth
study of the state of governance and local economic development in urban
and rural settings.

While conducting the field work, many Wereda administrators
expressed concern about using the population size of 100,000 inhabitants in

---

[5] This was recently established as a separate Woreda.

formulating government policy on decentralization and allocation of budgets. Many questioned the appropriateness of a decentralization program premised on such dubious figures. In discussions with Wereda administrators and executive committee members, it was pointed out that there were some Weredas with populations as big as 500,000, and suggestions were made that this be seriously considered in future policies. In addition, it was also repeatedly pointed out that increasing populations would likely give rise to more demands for further redivision of existing Weredas and creation of new ones; and this would have important implications for the allocation of budgets in the future. Be that as it may, however, it is important that regional and federal governments consider current and actual population sizes of Weredas in the process of allocating budgetary resources to different tiers of government.

7.2 Access to and Coverage of Public Services

One of the goals of a government's decentralization program is to increase the range and quality of public services in an accountable, responsive and transparent fashion. By the same token, one of the objectives of the Wereda decentralization study is to assess the level and distribution of social and economic services, such as education, health and clean water. As can be observed in table 2, field data have indicated important differences in the provision of social and economic services among the different Weredas. For example, Dera in Amhara, Yaya Gullele in Oromia, Silti in SNNPR and the two Weredas in Tigray region have been able to provide elementary and secondary education to more than 70% of those eligible for enrollment. On a comparative basis, Kilte Awlalo (75%) and Seharti-Samre (61%) have provided higher access to health services than all the other Weredas, which have only a relatively low but varying coverage ranging between 40%-61% of their populations. Generally, more people have got access to education than to health and clean water in all the Weredas sampled for this study.

In contrast to Weredas in the regions, residents in Arada and Addis Ketema Kifle Ketemas within Addis Ababa City Government have got the highest access to clean water and health and education services. This urban-rural disparity in access to services is a reflection of the situation at the national level, where, for example, access to improved water-drinking sources has reached 81% in urban areas and only 11% in rural areas (UNICEF 2006).

The reasons for the disparities in the provision of basic services among the different Weredas are not clear. Any possible set of reasons, including close monitoring of social and economic programs by the regional government; increased resource flows to Wereda governments; administrative capacities for implementing development programs; and/or political commitment by Wereda leaderships, can all account for the success in providing improved and better public services. Hence, it is suggested that an in-depth research be carried out to look into the factors that contribute to the success of Wereda administrations in providing efficient public services to their populations. The results of such investigation can serve policy aimed at promoting equitable provision of services and help individual Weredas to learn from best practices and exchange experiences on efficient and effective public services delivery programs.

Table 2. Selected indicators of access to public services in 8 Weredas and 2 Kifle Ketemas, 2006 (%age coverage)

No.	Name of Wereda/Kifle Ketema	Education	Health	Clean Water
1.	Dera	74.52	59.1	42.3
2.	Mecha	54.5	40.2	13.2
3.	Mullo-Sullulta	---	---	36.0
4.	Yaya Gullele	70.6	----	36.0
5.	Alaba	---	48.0	23.0
6.	Silti	81	54	---
7.	Kilte Awlalo	75	75	---
8.	Seharti-Samre	77	61	62
9.	Arada Kifle Ketema[6]	100	100	100
10.	Addis Ketema Kifle Ketema	100	95	NA

Source: Field data 2006.

7.3 Governance and Administrative Structure

According to data from the field study, the governance and administrative structure of Weredas consist of an executive committee, an elected council and a large pool of permanent personnel. The executive committee and the permanent cadre of employees work full time whereas the council is a semi-permanent assembly, which meets every three months to deliberate on the social and economic development plans of the Wereda government. It also has the authority to approve the Weredas' budgets and review the work progress of the different sector bureaus and the executive committees (i.e., the cabinets)

A Wereda is administered by an executive committee, otherwise known as the cabinet, whose membership can range between 11-13 elected members. The chairman of the executive committee is the chief administrator of the Wereda and the deputy usually serves as the vice-

---

[6] Given the rapid nature of the study, the 100% coverage rate could not be verified.

administrator and also heads the Wereda capacity building office. Most other members of the committee are heads of sector offices, such as education, health, agriculture and rural development, youth and social affairs, mass mobilization and public participation, etc. The executive committee is drawn from the Wereda council and is responsible for the day-to-day running of the economic and social matters of the Wereda. Being answerable to the council, its major function is to implement decisions and policies passed by the latter.

In Addis Ababa, Kifle Ketemas are run by care taker administrations appointed by the City Government of Addis Ababa to serve one-year tenures. The main responsibilities of these administrations are to: coordinate and execute social and economic development activities; ensure the continued implementation and execution of activities left behind from the previous administration; and, administer and decide upon the resources of the Kifle Ketemas, i.e., administer the budget and financial and human resources.

The direct appointment of care taker administrations, which are officially designated as 'neutral' in terms of their party affiliation, came in the aftermath of the unprecedented events of the May,2005, national elections that threw the country's electoral politics into turmoil. In the absence of elected urban councils, Kifle Ketema care taker administrations serve as both executive and deliberative (i.e., councils) bodies. In discussions with some members of care taker administrations, it was revealed that implementing decisions and orders from the central Addis Ababa City Government was their main preoccupation. The researchers were informed that there was very limited scope for independent decision making and planning at the Kifle Ketema level and upward accountability to higher officials rather than responsiveness to the needs and demands of the community characterized inter-governmental relations within the City Government of Addis Ababa.

The Wereda decentralization program does not recognize towns and cities as separate self-governing authorities. With the exception of some towns and cities in Tigray and Amhara, where municipal elections have been conducted following urban reform initiatives undertaken by the regional governments, the great majority of urban and semi-urban centers do not have elected municipal councils. As a result, Wereda administrators have been given the additional responsibility of supervising urban municipalities and semi-urban neighborhoods. This practice has put urban areas at a disadvantage because it may mean that urban services and development will be relegated to a secondary level. Equally important, since most municipalities do not have independent councils, decisions that affect cities/towns and semi-urban areas within the Wereda are made by the Wereda Council, whose membership is predominantly rural. Mayors and managers of such cities and rural townships are appointed by and are answerable to Wereda chief administrators, a practice which can generate more upward accountability at the cost of reduced responsiveness to the needs and concerns of urban communities.

Unlike Kifle Ketemas in Addis Ababa City Government, where appointed care taker administrations are operational, Wereda councils are elected bodies and their main function is to approve the budget and social and economic plans of the locality. As can be observed in table 3, council memberships range between 11-13 members. In the main, Wereda councils allocate block grants received from regional governments among sector programs. The councils are part-time, non-salaried deliberative bodies and meet 4 times a year to exercise oversight function over Wereda Executive Committees. According to the findings of this study, the present Wereda councilors came to office following the last local government elections in 2002/2003. Over the years, periodic by-elections have been frequently held to fill in seats left vacant due to different reasons, but no nationwide elections have been conducted since 2002/2003.

Table 3.   Composition of Wereda and Kifle Ketema Executive Committees (i.e., Cabinet) and Councils

No.	Name of Wereda	Wereda Executive Committee			Wereda Council		
		M	F	Total	M	F	Total
1.	Dera (Amhara)	11	1	12	-	-	87
2.	Mecha (Amhara)	10	1	11	92	22	114
3.	Mullo Sullulta (Oromia)	7	-	7	61	20	81
4.	Yaya Gullele (Oromia))	9	-	9	63	24	87
5.	Alaba (SNNPR)	10	1	11	221	4	225
6.	Silti (SNNPR)	12	1	13	74	34	108
7.	Kilte Awlalo (Tigray)	12	1	13	147	63	210
8.	Seharti-Samre (Tigray)	11	2	13	113	65	178
9.	Arada Kifle Ketema (Addis Ababa City Government)	6	4	2	NA	NA	NA
10.	Addis Ketema Kifle Ketema (Addis Ababa City Government)	5	3	2	NA	NA	NA

Source: Field data 2006.

NA = Not Applicable.

Based on table 3, the following observations can be made:

(a) The proportion of women in Wereda executive committees is infinitesimally small compared to the share of the female population as a percentage of total Wereda populations. Indeed, with the exception of Seharti-Samre, which has 2 women representatives, all the other executive committees have only 1 female member out of a total of 13 members. Mullo Sullulta and Yaya Gullele do not have any women on their executive committees. Major exceptions in this gender imbalance are the two sampled Kifle Ketemas in Addis Ababa, where women constitute between 33-44% of the leadership of the care taker administrations.

(b) There is a relatively better representation of women in Wereda Councils than in executive committees. Kilte Awlalo (43%) and Seharti-Samre (56%) Weredas in Tigray region have a much higher representation of women in the councils than any other Wereda. Other Weredas have female representations ranging between 24-46% of the total council membership. The notable exception is Alaba, which has less than 2% female representation in the council.

7.4 Level of Education of Wereda and Kifle Ketema Executive Committee Members

The shortage of personnel with sufficient educational qualifications and training is often cited as a major capacity constraint in advancing the Wereda decentralization agenda. This observation has particular relevance to Wereda executive committee members, who are key players in decision making and promoting good governance at the local level. Several studies indicate that the caliber of this category of personnel leaves much to be desired in terms of competence and experience in local self-government. What is needed, therefore, is an accelerated program of training to raise the level of expertise in many areas, including public services delivery, administration of local budgets and effective implementation of social and economic programs at the local level. It is with this view in mind that an assessment was conducted to look into the qualification and training levels of Wereda executive personnel. Table 4 presents a sample of the results.

As can be observed in table 4, there are differences in the levels of qualification and training of Wereda executive personnel. For example, Mecha, Dera, Kilte Awlalo and Seharti-Samre have more personnel with degree-level qualifications than Mullo Sullulta and Yaya Gulele. It can also be observed that most Wereda personnel hold diploma and certificate qualifications. Based on field data, it was learnt that most of these were former elementary and secondary school teachers with little or no formal training in the critical areas of public service delivery, good governance and local economic development. As was reiterated earlier, this makes it all the more urgent to launch an accelerated program of training to enhance the level of proficiency of Wereda personnel as key players in promoting good governance and local economic development.

Table 4. Educational qualification of Wereda and Kifle Ketema Executive
          Committee members

No.	Wereda	1st degree & above	College Diploma/ Certificate	High School Diploma	Below High School	Total
1.	Dera	4	7	1	-	12
2.	Mecha	4	6	-	1	11
3.	Mullo Sullulta	-	-	-	-	--
4.	Yaya Gullele	-	7	2	-	9
5.	Alaba	1	10	-	-	11
6.	Silti	1	11	-	1	13
7.	Kilte Awlalo	7	2	4	-	13
8.	Seharti-Samre	5	8	-	-	13
9.	Arada Kifle Ketema	5	1	-	-	6
10.	Addis Ketema Kifle Ketema	5	-	-	-	5

Source: Field data 2006.

The caliber and level of education of personnel of the caretaker administrations of the 2 Kifle Ketemas in Addis Ababa City Government is by far higher than any of the Weredas from the regions. This is understandable in view of the fact that the personnel serving in the caretaker administrations are appointed by the Addis Ababa City Government ostensibly to serve for one year under the close supervision and direction of the central administration.

7.5 Party Politics in Wereda Government

Competitive party politics at the local level is an essential element in democratic governance. One of the great advantages of different parties acting at the local level is that they can offer different policy and program choices to citizens; and widen the political space for different actors to participate in economic and political decision making. An open political process that allows open policy debates and free flow of alternative ideas by state and non-state actors is necessary for the institutionalization of a democratic culture. This should be an unequivocal commitment of any government aspiring to build a democratic and participatory political order. Party politics in Ethiopian local government must be assessed against this important parameter.

As in many other systems, party politics is an important aspect of local governments in Ethiopia, and permeates many aspects of Wereda administration, particularly recruitment and appointment to leadership roles. However, the state of local politics and governance is far from being competitive because of the domineering presence of the EPRDF as the sole party managing state-society relations at the local level. According to research findings, EPRDF membership has become the single most important criterion to assume a leadership position in Wereda governance. In discussions with administrators and sector office heads, it was also pointed out that executive committees, which are key actors in political and economic matters affecting the community, are all occupied by persons who are members of the ruling EPRDF. In group discussions and field interviews, it was also disclosed that key sector offices, such as finance and economic development and mass mobilization and capacity building, were most often headed by people who are members of the ruling party. Apart from giving particular advantages to the party in power, single party dominance of the Wereda government political landscape does not augur well for competitive politics and participatory governance at the local level.

The domination of the Wereda government scene by the ruling party has its pros and cons. On the positive side, it means that the government has strong leverage at the local level to insure the effective implementation of party/government programs and policies. On the negative side, it has the danger of encouraging upward accountability to regional and federal politics at the cost of community needs and concerns. Equally important, single party supremacy in Wereda government can mean the narrowing of the political space for non-ruling party actors and severe limitations on opposition political parties to operate freely and provide alternative social and economic programs for the community. It needs no reminding also that pervasive party control of executive leaderships and important sector offices will most likely result in the disappearance of the distinction between government and party functions at the Wereda level-- a situation that will favor the ruling party in very many ways.

7.6 Wereda and Kifle Ketema Administrative Personnel

In addition to executive committees and councils, there is a large pool of permanent and contract administrative personnel that constitute part of the governance and administrative structure of Wereda governments. The key role of the permanent staff is to assist in the delivery of public services and carrying out social and economic programs at the local level. In group discussions and interviews with administrators and councilors, it was repeatedly pointed out that most employees were underpaid and have low educational qualifications. They lacked core skills in basic management, finance, planning and public services delivery. It was suggested that Wereda personnel be given diversified training in participatory budgeting, report writing, basic accounting and financial management, planning and managing micro-finance schemes and small projects/enterprises; and community empowerment strategies to enhance their proficiency in local economic development.

Table 5. Permanent and contract employees of selected Weredas and Kifle Ketemas

No.	Name of Wereda	Number of Employees		Total
		Male	Female	
1.	Dera	707	394	1101
2.	Mecha	987	652	1639
3.	Mullo Sullulta	-	-	351
4.	Alaba	766	44	810
5.	Kilte Awlalo	473	389	862
6.	Seharti-Samre	812	287	1099
7.	Arada Kifle Ketema	---	---	---
8.	Addis Ketema Kifle Ketema	872	986	1,858

Source: Field data 2006.

As can be observed in table 5, most Weredas have a sizable labor force that can be harnessed to promote local economic development and increase the scale and efficiency of public services. The number of employees varies across Weredas. For example, Mecha in Amhara with 1,639 employees and Seharti-Samre in Tigray with 1,099 employees top the list while Mullo Sullulta in Oromia with 351 employees has the least number of employees. It was not clear whether the difference in the number of employees among Weredas could be attributed to population size or any other relevant factor. It is important to note that Kilte Awlalo and Mecha with 45% and 40%, respectively, have the highest percentage of female employees. Alaba with only 5% of total employees being female, shows the lowest female representation among the sampled Weredas.

According to research findings, the bulk of Wereda permanent personnel were elementary and secondary school teachers. For example, in Alaba out of the entire labor force of about 766 employees, 565 or nearly 74% were teachers while the rest could be classified into different administrative personnel. As will be explained elsewhere in this article, salaries for teachers consume a disproportionately high share of the Weredas' annual budgets, leaving very little for expansion of public services and local economic development.

Wereda administrators and councilors repeatedly pointed out that there were many vacant positions that remained unfilled in their respective Weredas; and this would have serious repercussions on their capacities to deliver services and undertake local economic development. Two reasons were given for this state of affairs. First, Weredas frequently experience severe budgetary limitations that have crippled efforts to hire badly needed personnel, particularly in the technical areas of infrastructure expansion and services. Second, low salaries and poor benefits have rendered Wereda governments less competitive in attracting and retaining required personnel. Current labor shortages in the market and reluctance of potential recruits to serve in Weredas with poor services and facilities were also cited as additional reasons that exacerbated the problem.

Addis Ketema Kifle Ketema has a large labor force of 1,858 permanent and contract employees consisting mainly of civil servants, teachers and health professionals. Field data provided by the Kifle Ketema indicated that 986 employees or 53% of the total labor force were women. Most of the employees are deployed in the 9 kebeles that come under the jurisdiction of the administration of the Kifle Ketemas.

7.7 Inter-Governmental Relations

As was explained in the background section of this paper, Ethiopia has a 5-tier system of government: federal, regional, zonal, wereda and kebele levels of administration. The formal powers and responsibility of each of these tiers of government are defined by law.

For example, according to the federal constitution, local government is the responsibility of regional governments, which have been given the power to determine the authority and functions of any sub-national governments, such as Weredas or Kebele administrations, that will be established within the regions. Be that as it may, however, a distinction has to be made between the formal definition of powers and functions of the different levels of government and the actual practice in inter-governmental relations. Simply put, actual inter-governmental functional and authority relationships may not be in accord with the spirit and meaning of the law or may be quite different from what is prescribed in the law or the constitution of the country. It is, therefore, necessary that generalizations about the actual working of inter-governmental relations be based not solely on what the legislation says but on how the different levels of government operate on the ground and relate to each other.

As was mentioned elsewhere in this article, it was observed that zonal administrations have an independent legal existence and formally recognized role only in SNNPR. They are full-fledged tiers of local government with their own elected councils, executive administrations and separate budgets. Although not formally recognized tiers of government, zonal administrations in other regions exert considerable degrees of influence on Wereda administrations by providing administrative support in preparing budgets and business process re-engineering plans. Because of shortage of competent personnel experienced by Wereda Administrations, zonal administrations play important roles in the administration and governance of the Wereda levels of government in the many regions of the country.

According to research findings, the lines of authority and accountability between Wereda and regional governments are not clearly defined. Much of the functional and authority relationships are largely governed by political considerations rather than by a clearly defined set of authority and accountability parameters at each level of government. As a result, although the law recognizes the formal independence of each tier of government, the governmental structure is generally characterized by top-down modes of control and supervision. According to the law, for example, Weredas are formally declared to be independent local government authorities but in reality there is a great deal of supervision and control by regional and federal governments over Wereda affairs. In the Ethiopian situation where local governments are heavily dependent on regional and central governments for budgets and single-party dominance in local government is highly visible, the independence and autonomy of Wereda governments as well as their accountability and responsiveness to local communities will leave much to be desired. The preceding generalizations pertaining to Wereda-regional inter-governmental relations equally apply to Wereda-Kebele inter-governmental relations.

8. Budget Administration in Wereda Government

In Ethiopia, block grants are the principal means by which regional governments transfer resources to Wereda governments; and as such, constitute the lion's share of Wereda budgets. Block grant decisions by regional governments are made on the basis of a set of criteria, which consisted of 4 variables: population (55%); development index (25%); revenue sharing effort (15%); and poverty level index (10%) (Tegegne and

Kassahun 2006). It is the responsibility of Wereda councils to allocate these grants to different sectoral programs, such as education, health, rural development, etc., most often on the basis of directives received from regional and zonal administrations.

Table 6 presents annual budgets of sampled Weredas for 3 years covering the period 1996-1998 E.C. In focus group discussions and field interviews, administrators and councilors pointed out that on average more than 95% of Wereda budgets were made up of grants received from regional governments. This is a clear indication of the heavy financial dependence of Wereda governments on regional and central governments. It is also a stark reminder of the narrow revenue base of Wereda administrations. In field discussions, it was also disclosed that Wereda governments had very little say on the amount of block grants received which were hardly enough for financing services and local economic development for the full year.

Table 6. Annual Budgets of 8 Weredas, 1996/1998 E.C. (in Birr/millions)

No.	Wereda	Total Annual Budgets			3-year average % share of administrative and operational expenditures
		1996	1997	1998	
1.	Dera	8.49	12.42	12.08	85
2.	Mecha	11.47	-----	12.47	--
3.	Mullo Sullulta	7.14	8.43	9.15	94
		(1995)	(1996)	(1997)	
4.	Yaya Gullele	3.32	4.98	6.24	93
5.	Alaba	2.46	2.45	1.85	85
6.	Silti	5.90	6.81	8.41	96
7.	Kilte Awlalo	5.12	7.10	9.51	99
8.	Seharti-Samre	8.59	9.36	11.19	88

Source: Field data 2006.

Based on table 6, it can be observed that on average 91% of Weredas' annual budgets are earmarked for administrative and operational expenditures. During focus group discussions, it was revealed that the largest chunk of this expenditure went to salaries for teachers, health workers and personnel working in Wereda administrative offices. This situation left Wereda governments with very little for undertaking capital projects and expanding public services. Apart from budget shortfalls, a recurring major challenge afflicting many Wereda governments was found to be assignment of increasing functions and responsibilities without the financial wherewithal to live up to the expectations that Wereda decentralization had created among the community.

9.   Findings and Observations

This section discusses preliminary findings and observations drawn on the basis of the field investigation and interviews and focus group discussions with Wereda executive committee members and councilors as well as some members of 2 Kifle Ketemas in Addis Ababa City government. The issues raised here will serve as important points of departure for the research proposal for a comprehensive and in-depth study of Wereda-level decentralization.

a)   Shrinking political space

Based on field findings, the ruling EPRDF has a heavy presence at the level of Wereda government in many aspects; and this has led to the shrinking of the political space for non-state actors to fully participate in economic and political issues affecting the locality. One indication of single party dominance is the fact that all Wereda cabinet members and most councilors are members of the ruling EPRDF party. It was also the case that party membership was increasingly becoming an important consideration in holding important administrative and political positions in Wereda government. The absence of a leveling field for non-ruling party actors and civil society organizations cannot advance competitive politics and can be a brake on participatory governance. One-party monopoly of the political landscape at the local level will also have important implications on the autonomy of Wereda governments and generate risks of more upward accountability at the cost of reduced responsiveness and answerability to the community.

b)   Increased demands for services

In the various focus group discussions and interviews, it was repeatedly pointed out that Wereda-level decentralization has given rise to increased demands for more social and economic services, such as education, health, clean water and rural roads. Weredas have not been able to meet the expectations of the community due to inadequate finances and shortage of skilled local government personnel capable of delivering efficient services. To satisfy the demand for more services, it may be necessary to increase inter-governmental resource transfers side by side with an effective campaign to mobilize local resources for implementing new development projects and increasing the range and quality of public services.

c) The problem of unfunded mandates

According to field findings, it was reported that Wereda governments constantly faced the problem of unfunded mandates. The problem was created because regional and federal governments routinely assigned functions to Weredas without adequate resources to carry out the tasks. Ideally, mandates must be accompanied with adequate resources, i.e. skilled personnel, money, equipment and vehicles, to carry them out. Many administrators also reiterated the fact that mandates without the needed resources had created public mistrust and led to cynicism about the ability of local government to deliver on its promises.

d) Disproportionate share of salaries and administrative expenditures in Wereda budgets

In almost all Weredas sampled for the study, salaries and other administrative expenditures constituted the lion's share of their budgets. This had left Weredas with little for capital/development projects and expansion of services. In practice, the block grants that Weredas received from regional governments and allocated among various budget items had on several occasions proved inadequate to meet the increasing service demands of the community.

e) Severe capacity constraints at the Wereda level

Apart from budgetary and financial problems, severe shortages or lack of competent and trained personnel stood out as a key constraint for effective Wereda decentralization in this country. In addition, shortages of equipment, such as computers, printers and other office supplies were frequently cited as recurring problems. The problems got more serious in remote and inaccessible Weredas, which were far removed from the attention of the regions and where it was extremely difficult to recruit people that would be willing to serve in these areas. In the focus group discussions with administrators, it was suggested that regional governments might have to introduce special incentive packages, for example, higher pay and attractive allowances, to lure people to work in undeveloped and remote Weredas where people were generally reluctant to go to.

f) Absence of legal/regulatory framework for implementation of Wereda decentralization policy

It was observed in the field that a legal/regulatory framework for implementation of the Wereda decentralization program was missing in many regions. Apart from the regional constitutions, which state formal powers of the regional and Wereda governments, there is no detailed legislation which defined key issues in inter-governmental relations, such as Wereda-regional government jurisdictions and extent of financial and revenue autonomy of Wereda governments. Although some regions have taken limited initiatives in this regard, for example, the draft local finance bill by the Amhara region, most other regions had not paid sufficient attention to this critical policy element in the effective institutionalization of the Wereda decentralization program.

g) Limited devolution of power and functions to Kebeles

Kebeles are the lowest tiers of government in the state structure very close to the people. As such, they should be provided with sufficient decision-making autonomy, administrative competencies and adequate resources to address the demands and concerns of the community. It was, however, observed that sufficient decision-making authority, responsibilities and resources had not been devolved to Kebele levels of administration to empower them to live up to the expectations of the people for more and improved services. In reality, Kebeles most often operated as recipients and implementers of decisions and orders from Wereda governments rather than semi-independent institutions of self-government and empowerment at the grassroots level. In addition, there were complaints that Kebele administrations did not receive sufficient budget to provide services and this had meant that their activities were hamstrung by close control and monitoring by Wereda governments.

10. Conclusion

The Wereda-level decentralization program was officially launched in 2002/03 in 430 Weredas in the 4 major regions --- Amhara, Oromia, SNNPR and Tigray. The Government's official intent was to devolve governmental power and resources to Weredas in order to make them vehicles for democratic governance and participatory development. Over the past couple of years, however, the process of pushing down authority, responsibility and resources to Weredas has not been successfully carried out. Institutional and resource constraints, including lack of experience in decentralized governance, insufficient and weak revenue base, shortage of skilled personnel to manage public services, limited public involvement in local economic development and an entrenched political culture of top-down decision-making and governance structure, have all held back the institutionalization of an effective system of decentralization.

Local government finance is the key to a successful decentralization program. In general, the more financial autonomy a local government unit has, the greater its decision-making authority to focus on local concerns and priorities. The Ethiopian reality does not fit into this observation because Wereda governments are heavily dependent on regional governments for budgets, which come in the form of block grants using a set of criteria. Although Wereda councils have the formal legal authority to allocate block grants amongst different sectoral programs, the actual disbursement of the resources and important decisions on allocations are greatly influenced by directives that originate from the regional and federal governments. Under such a scenario, it can be argued that regional and federal government priorities will take precedence over local community needs and preferences.

Wereda decentralization has empowered local communities to make decisions on matters of concern to the community. However, there are caveats to this observation. Among other things, this assertion has been circumvented by the dominance of the Wereda government landscape by the ruling EPRDF party, which has resulted in the narrowing of the political space for non-ruling party actors and civil society organizations. Obviously, this state of affairs will have serious long-term implications for the institutionalization of democratic and participatory governance at the local level. Simply put, the perpetuation of one-party rule can deprive the people of the right to exercise judgment on different economic and political alternatives --- a far cry from competitive politics at the local level.

The past few years have brought out the challenges of effective Wereda decentralization. The problems of unfunded mandates; a high proportion of local budgets going to cover salaries and administrative expenditures leaving little for expanding public services; heavy financial dependence of local authorities on the federal government; and a dearth of skilled personnel have been principal constraints militating against the institutionalization of an effective system of Wereda government. One should not also lose sight of the fact that an authoritarian political culture and a long tradition of central government dominance in matters which can legitimately be left to local jurisdictions have also been contributory factors to lack of much needed progress in Wereda decentralization.

References

Andargatchew Tiruneh. 1993. *The Ethiopian Revolution: A transformation from an aristocratic to a totalitarian autocracy.* Cambridge: Cambridge University Press.

Asmelash Beyene. 1987. Some notes on the evolution of regional administration in Ethiopia. *Ethiopian Journal of Development Research,* Vol. 9, No.1 (April). Addis Ababa: Institute of Development Research, Addis Ababa University.

_____. 2000. Decentralization as a tool for resolving the nationality problem: The Ethiopian experience. 2000. *Regional Development Dialogue,* Vol. 21, No. 1 (Spring).

CIDA. 2005. Ethiopia: Institutional governance review – grassroots empowerment: Review of progress and prospects. Addis Ababa, Ethiopia, October.

Clapham, Christopher. 1969. *Haile Selassie's government.* New York: Praeger.

_____. 1988. *Transformation and continuity in revolutionary Ethiopia.* Cambridge: Cambridge University Press.

Central Statistical Authority (CSA). 2004. *Statistical Abstract.* Addis Ababa: CSA.

Department for International Development (DFID). 2003. Government of Ethiopia: Review of capacity building approaches for local government in Ethiopia. Draft Report. Development in Practice Ltd. Nottingham, United Kingdom.

Dessalegn Rahmato. 1984. Agrarian reform in Ethiopia. Uppsala: Scandinavian Institute of African Studies.

Dessalegn Rahmato and Meheret Ayenew. 2005. *Democracy assistance to post-conflict Ethiopia: Building local institutions.'* Clingendael: Netherlands Institute of International Relations; Addis Ababa: Forum for Social Studies.

Fenta Mandefro. 1999. Decentralization in post-Derg Ethiopia: Aspects of Federal-Regional relations. Masters Thesis. Regional and Local Development Studies, Addis Ababa University, Addis Ababa.

Federal Democratic Republic of Ethiopia (FDRE). 1995. A Proclamation of the Constitution of the Federal Democratic Republic of Ethiopia', Negarit Gazetta, 1st year, No. 1, Addis Ababa.

Fukui. K., and J. Markakis. 1994. *Ethnicity and conflict in the Horn of Africa.* Athens: Ohio University Press.

Koehn, Peter. 1974. Jurisdiction of local government with particular reference to municipalities in Ethiopia. In *Studies in Ethiopian government and administration.* Faculty of Arts, Haile Selassie I University, Addis Ababa.

Lissane Yohannes and Mohammed Mussa. 2005. Assessment of district level decentralization and capacity building in Tigray, Amhara, Oromiya and SNNP Regional States. DFID, Addis Ababa, December.

Meheret Ayenew. 1998. Some preliminary observations on institutional and administrative gaps in Ethiopia's decentralization processes. Working Paper No.1 (September). Regional and Local Development Studies, Addis Ababa University, Addis Ababa, Ethiopia.

_____. 2002. Decentralization in Ethiopia: Two case studies of devolution of power and responsibilities to local government authorities in Ethiopia. In *Ethiopia: The challenge of democracy from below,* edited by Bahru Zewde and Siegfreid Pausewang. Uppsala: Nordiska Afrikainstitutet; Addis Ababa: Forum for Social Studies.

Rondinelli, D., and G.S. Cheema. 1983. *Decentralization in developing countries: Review of recent experience.* Vol. 581. Washington, D.C: World Bank.

Slater, David. 1989. Territorial power and the peripheral State: The issue of decentralization. *Development and Change*, Vol. 20. London: Sage.

Smith, B.C. 1985. Decentralization: *The territorial dimension of the state.* London: George Allen and Unwin.

Tegegne, G.E. and Kassahun Berhanu. 2006. Decentralization in Ethiopia: Literature Review. Forum for Social Studies, November.

Transitional Government of Ethiopia (TGE). 1992. A Proclamation to Provide for the Establishment of National/Regional Self-Governments, Negarit Gazetta, 51st Year, No. 7, Addis Ababa, Ethiopia.

UNICEF-Ethiopia. 2006. Water, environment and sanitation – action. Addis Ababa, Ethiopia.

World Bank. 2001. Ethiopia: Woreda studies, Vol.1, November. Ethiopia Country Office.

Annex I

List of Focus Group Discussants and Interviewees

Addis Ababa City Government

1. Ato Sewagene Delele, Head, Health and Social Affairs Department, Addis Ketema Kifle Ketema

2. Ato Anteneh Mitiku, Head, Health Department, Addis Ababa Kifle Ketema

3. Ato Fisseha Tedla, Head, Education Desk, Arada Kifle Ketema

Amhara Region

1. Ato Sematchew Nigatu, D/Head, Capacity Building Bureau

2. Ato Nigatu Alamirew, Head, Administration, Mecha Wereda

3. Ato Mulatu Worke, Expert, Civil Service Reform, Mecha

4. Ato Wuletaw Awoke, Head, Civil Service Desk, Dera Wereda

5. Ato Worku Kinde, Head, Health Office, Dera

6. Ato Melesse Ayele, Inspector, Civil Service, Dera

7. Ato Shumet Ambaw, Head, Education Office, Dera

8. Ato Ibrahim Mohammed, Head, Administration, Dera

9. Ato Mulugeta Zeleke, Head, Dera Wereda Budget Desk

Oromia Region

1. Ato Seyoum Hailu, Chief Administrator, Mullo Sullulta Wereda

2. Ato Fekadu Abera, Deputy Administrator, Mullo Sullulta

3. Ato Teketel Abebe, Senior Plan Expert, Mullo Sullulta

4. Ato Teshome Garedew, Chief Administrator, Yaya Gullele Wereda

5. Ato Gizachew Girma, Head, Rural and Agricultural Development Office, Yaya Gullele

6. Ato Girma Haile Selassie, Head, Rural and Agricultural Development Office, Yaya Gullele

7. Ato Kebabaw Adamu, Speaker, Wereda Council, Yaya Gullele

8. Ato Neway Wondimu, Wereda Education Office, Representative, Yaya Gullele

9. Ato Gashaw Seyoum, Head, Public Relations and Information, Yaya Gullele

10. Ato Girma Ayele, Inspector, Health Office, Yaya Gullele Wereda

11. Ato Deme Birru, Deputy Administrator and Head, Capacity Building, Yaya Gullele

SNNPR

1. Ato Bateno Ahmed, Chief Administrator, Alaba Special Wereda

2. Ato Nuredin Hasse, D/Administrator, Alaba Special Wereda

3. Ato Bedru Hasse, Head, Education Bureau

4. Ato Sanni Reddi, Chief Administrator, Silti Zone

5. Ato Mustafa Adem, Chief Administrator, Silti Zone

Tigray Region

1. Ato Gidey G/Yohannes, Head, Capacity Building Bureau, Tigray Region

2. Ato Ammanuel G/Tensae, D/Head of Bureau,   >>

3. Ato Zekarias Kiros, Head, Capacity Building, Kilte Awlalo

4. Ato Wozam Alemu, Head, Security and Public Mobilization, Kilte Awlalo

5. Ato Tesfaye Aberra, D/Administrator, Kilte Awlalo

6. Ato Kalaeyu G/Hiwot, Head, Wereda Administration, Kilte Awlalo

7. Ato Mammo Gebre-Egziabher, Chief Wereda Administrator, Kilte Awlalo

8. Ato Mehari G/Medhin, head, Agricultural and Rural Development, Kilte Awlalo

9. Ato Abreha Berhe, Speaker, Wereda Council, Kilte Awlalo

10. Ato Abreha Yirgaw, Head, Trade and Industry Office, Kilte Awlalo

11. Ato Suleiman Adem, Chief Administrator, Seharti-Samre.

III

Decentralized Governance and Service Delivery: A Case Study of Digelu and Tijo Wereda of Arsi Zone in Oromia Region[*]

Kumera Kanea Tucho

1. Introduction

Currently there is a global trend towards entrenching decentralized governance systems. Since the late 1980s, decentralized form of governance is gaining currency as a strategy for political and economic development in developing countries. With changes in development theories and policy prescriptions, there has been a significant shift from mechanistic and top-down models towards more dynamic, bottom-up and participatory approaches through different reform measures including decentralization.

One of the factors that led to adopting decentralization has been the realization of the difficulty to manage a country's political, social and economic activities only from the center. This is because of the weak performance of past development approaches. Concentration of decision-making powers at central level resulted in delays in implementation of activities at local level. The center has increasingly proved to possess neither the capacity nor the time to deal with all issues surrounding services and local development, which could be better handled at the local level. This is compounded by ineffective local institutions and lack of participation on the part of beneficiaries. Such institutional problems together with other factors led to economic crisis and the taking shape of conflicts in different countries, which in turn, led to the necessity of decentralized approaches. Therefore, most countries are experiencing some form of decentralization characterized by both differing and similar objectives. Among these objectives, delivery of basic services at the local level is one of the motives that propel the drive towards a decentralized governance system.

---

[*] This chapter is based on the author's MA Thesis submitted to the Institute of Regional and Local Development Studies, Addis Ababa University, 2006.

This trend is a recent phenomenon in Ethiopia. Since 1991, a series of reform measures were introduced in the country to effectively institute a multi-faceted decentralized system first at regional and subsequently at *wereda* level. With the adoption of a decentralized approach, it was expected that the system would create local governments, which are more accountable to their constituencies aimed at enhancing self-reliance, democratic decision-making, and citizen participation. Provision of public services through decentralized institutions and participation of the population has also the advantage of matching local needs and priorities with required resources.

However, delivering basic services is still posing significant challenges. Basic service provision is at a very low stage of development. The coverage of education, health, water supply, roads and other facilities is very low and the majority of the population faces difficulties in getting access to such services. Though gross enrollment increased in the education sector, there are still challenges in addressing the problem. The Welfare Monitoring Survey Report (CSA 2004) shows that gross enrollment ratio at the primary level has shown improvement. The ratio increased from 37.4 percent in 1996 to 74.2 percent in 2004. The number of dropouts has declined from 18.5 to 13.6 percent during the same period, but the report indicates that there are still challenges in meeting the required number of classrooms, teachers and textbooks. According to the report the major problem in the health sector is supply of health personnel and drugs. It is also indicated that vaccination coverage for children under five years is below 60 percent. In terms of water supply also, 64 percent of the population are reported as using unclean drinking water. This problem is more severe in rural areas as 74.5 percent of the rural population has no access to clean water. The report of the Ministry of Water Resources (June 2005) also shows that only 35 percent of the rural population has access to clean drinking water while the coverage in urban areas is 82 percent. In terms of access to road the Welfare Monitoring Survey indicates that around 58 percent of rural households travel five or more kilometers to reach the nearest all-weather road. On the other hand, population growth is expanding at an alarming rate thereby making the challenges faced in service delivery more complex. Owing to this, the situation in rural Ethiopia merits focus and attention as regards service delivery in the drive towards poverty reduction. Hence, this chapter reviews the performance and constraints of selected public services in the sectors of education, health, water supply and rural roads in view of wereda decentralization. The article is part of the result of study conducted in Digelu and Tijo wereda of Oromia region, which assessed the performance of the wereda in view of decentralized service delivery.

2. Theoretical Framework

Services are extraordinary heterogeneous and there is no clear boundary to demarcate goods from services. Some times both terms are used interchangeably. It also varies from private goods to public goods (Barlow 1981, 81-2; Bailey 1999, 48). In general, services are acknowledged as constituting a category of public goods which are related with sectoral development issues and defined as basic developmental goods or services and contribute to human needs or development. Delivery of such services could follow different arrangements or models varying between the continuums of purely private to purely public, with numerous hybrid cases in between involving different agencies such as the private sector, NGOs, lower tiers of government and communities or households. Hence, a country may organize service delivery in a variety of ways and levels ranging from private to public and from highly centralized to highly decentralized level (World Development Report 2004).

Centralization refers to the concentration of authority or decision-making powers on a wide range of issues in a central body/entity. This entails the holding of power at the central level. Until the end of the 1960s, the centralized state used to have an expanding role in the operation of the economy and governments assumed dominant or monopolistic roles in providing public services, including education, health, social security and macroeconomic management (Munday 1996, 97; Dunleavy & O'leary 1981; World Development Report 1997, 100-105; Goss 2001). However, with the mounting economic problems during the critical periods of the 1970s and 1980s, the centralized states, particularly those in developing countries, began to face difficult challenges of inefficiency including the provision of basic services to their citizens. The challenge of the time prompted a debate beyond national boundaries, both in development thought and policy circles leading to successive shifts of policy as expressed in different reform measures (Martinussen 1997, 257). Consequently, the traditional state has been expressed as an institution with complex and ineffective government institutions characterized by bureaucratic red tape, delays, communication overload and distortion of information, and principal-agent hierarchical political power structures. Under the centralized system, the mission of service providers and what is provided is determined centrally without involvement of the public at grassroots or community level. Priorities are set by centralized institutions that are unresponsive to local needs and unaccountable to local constituents, thus resulting in inadequate provision commensurate with local conditions. Nor has the centralized form of service delivery been capable of discharging its responsibilities to fulfill these needs (Chikulo 1998, 9; Senboja & Therkildsen 1995, 1-3; Hailu 2003). According to Elcak (1994,

109-111), this is because of the limitation of the state, the inefficiency and ineffectiveness of state services to meet public needs owing to lack of resources and other capacities and the evolution of new approaches for service delivery such as privatization and expansion of other local actors in providing services.

However, the private sector in developing countries is at its infant stage and its capacity to provide the wide range of public services will remain very low contrary to the aspirations of the proponents of the market. In the case of developing countries, the problem of affordability is also an issue. Under this circumstance, government intervention safeguards the interest of the poor through equitable distribution of resources for providing public services and in availing services that are not made available by the private sector to enable equitable and uniform service provision irrespective of socio-economic category of customers or consumers (Streeten 1995, 200-203). This required a new arrangement through decentralized governance system in which both the public and the private sector can operate either jointly or independently in the process of providing efficient services.

Therefore, the issue is not only a question of state or market preference but also a governance issue that brings all central and local actors together towards the goal of providing improved services. Governance is an emerging field in development discourse that is gaining significance since the 1990s. It comprises *the set of values, rules, policies, institutions, practice,* actors, processes and traditions, regulations and laws *by which a society manages its economic, political and social affairs through interactions among the government, civil society and the private sector.* Thus, governance includes the mode and manner of instituting a government in the management of a country's or society's affairs. It determines how power is exercised, how decisions are taken and how citizens have their say on matters affecting them. It is also concerned with the legitimacy of officials and institutions in ensuring effective delivery of public services (UNDP 2000, 26; Bahatta 1998, 186; Olowu 2000, 5-6; Mugerwa 2003, 16). It is a manner in which authority is organized and exercised or the way a society organizes itself to make and implement decisions through mutual understanding, agreement and action (Goss 2001, 11; Tegegne and Kassahun 2004, 37).

The issue of governance has been considered as a missing link in the first and second-generation of the stabilization and structural adjustment reforms and many reasons could be attributed to the need for a reform agenda under governance realm. Among these, the unrealized hopes of the developmental state, fiscal crises and economic decline, war and the wave of democratic reforms, the unrealizable prescriptions of SAPs, and conditions put by donors, that required reduction of domestic corruption and the need for increased political participation are the main arguments advanced for the reform agenda. The pressure exerted by globalization has also pushed the governments of developing countries to improve their governance image particularly in attracting foreign direct investments (Mugerwa 2003; World Development Report 1997, 120; Chikulo 1998, 81; UN-HABITAT 2002, 20; Hamdok 2003, 20-21). This necessitated the existence of effective domestic institutions marked by efficiency, participation, accountability, transparency, the rule of law, and political pluralism in which service delivery is enhanced by increased public sector efficiency. Recently these features, or attributes of governance are considered to prevail under decentralized governance system particularly in a devolved form of decentralization.(Doornbos 2000, 189-191; Mugerwa 2003, 17).

Though the concept of decentralization has been around for long, it has reemerged as a condition for achieving sustainable socio-economic development and as fundamental goal in democratic governance since the 1980s (Chikulo, 1998: 84-85). Tegegne and Kassahun (2004, 36) defined the concept as the transfer of legal and political authority from a central government and its affiliates to sub-national units of government in the process of making decisions and managing public functions. This definition is more or less made in the context of devolution which is the most extensive form of decentralization that involves far more radical approach that confers full authority and responsibility to discharge specified functions upon formally constituted autonomous local agencies that can operate independently in their own areas of jurisdiction (Martinussen, 1997:211; Chikulo 1998, 93). Contrary to the practice under other forms of decentralization, devolved local governments have clear and legally recognized geographic boundaries and over which they exercise authority and within which they perform public functions. It enables sub-national units to raise revenue and make independent investment decision in providing public services (Turner and Hulme 1997, 154). Since authority is vested in representatives elected by the local population, devolved political sub-divisions such as regional authorities or local authorities are politically responsible to the local population, for their decisions and their activities are substantially outside the direct control of central government. Hence, a devolved form of decentralization has been favored as the most efficient approach in public service delivery characterized by better coordination, efficient and effective mobilization and utilization of resources, participation, attainment of local priorities and preferences and accountability. This lent decentralization worldwide recognition as the most significant model for better delivery of public services and enhancement of economic development.

Contrary to reliance on central governments, which is characterized by longer delays and greater costs of administration, decentralization divides and disperses services that are provided from the center to local levels. It reduces workload and congestion in the channels of administration and communication and enhances better coordination of functions much more quickly than it happens at the central bureaucracies and offers the chance for efficient, flexible and responsive services (Osborne and Gaebler 1992, 168-169; World Development Report 1997, 122; Chukilo 1998, 91).

Decentralization is also argued as the best approach in enhancing popular participation and became one of the strategies in attaining the objective of increasing popular participation and management of economic and social development. It has been considered as a means of empowering people so that they are able to initiate actions on their own from below and thus influence the processes and outcomes of development by shifting the focus of development from above (from central planning and bureaucratic government agencies) to community-based participatory systems that use the full range of local, public and private institutions (Turner and Hulme 1997, 113-114). Particularly, under the framework of a devolved system of decentralization, it is believed that participation is effective and enables local communities or people at grassroots level to influence policies that affect their daily lives including the setting of local taxes, and provision of social services (Kibre 1994; Bulti 1994, 144). It places more power and resources at a closer, more familiar, and more easily influenced level of government. It creates opportunities for citizen-state interaction in which people gain voice in critical decisions and will increasingly apply pressure from below for power and resources to ensure improvements in their access to resources and services (Streeten 1995, 256; Tegegne and Kassahun 2004, 35).

By devolving decision-making powers to local governments, decentralization can also generate financial capacities, efficiency and quality gains that promote effective delivery of services. It entails shifting of responsibilities with corresponding fiscal resources to sub-national levels and allows not only increased resource mobilization but also maximizes the provision of services by allowing local governments to take decisions on the allocation of scarce resources, according to local needs and priorities (World Bank 1999/2000, 108; Martinussen 1997, 213). In this case it approaches a competitive market in that local governments supply services on the basis of people's preferences, tastes and needs and people are made to pay a tax based on the benefit they receive (Van der Loop 2002, 46). It allows equal participation by different actors and helps to focus mainly on the avoidance of unnecessary and wasteful use of public resources and in cost minimization and better allocation system in the effort of achieving the objective of public service delivery. When resources are scarce and less cost effective, priorities will be better adopted to local conditions and locally perceived needs and public service delivery systems will be flexible and suited to local needs. This is due to the fact that local governments have informational advantages over the central government. Locally elected leaders and local institutions are closer to the people and they know the situation in their locality than authorities at national level and are in a better position to provide services needed by local people. They are also in a better position to secure the public participation in identification, prioritization, approval and implementation of public services (World Development Report 1999/2000, 108; Tegegne and Asfaw 2002). Local communities also have a better experience and knowledge about their environment and can therefore better identify their development needs and potential, and initiate development activities that address their needs. This permits and enables decisions to be made locally and closer to the communities with better information and local knowledge, and better coordination. Therefore, being aware of local conditions and needs, local politicians and civil servants will be more responsive to citizens' preferences than the central government which tends to provide the same level of public services throughout the country regardless of differences in tastes from one locality to the other (Gant 1979, 169; Turner and Hulme 1997, 157; Bulti 1994,150).

Decentralization is also argued as a mechanism to enhance accountability for service delivery by enforcing accountability relationship among policy makers, service providers and service receivers. Therefore, it encourages greater accountability at the local level and increases the accountability of government to the people by increasing the responsiveness of local institutions. In this regard, Turner and Hulme (1997, 157) and Meheret (1998, 5) also argue that accountability is enhanced because local representatives are more accessible to the populace and can thus be held more closely accountable for their policies and outcomes than distant authorities at the central level. Physical proximity also makes it easy to hold local officials accountable for their performance.

3. Institutional Arrangements for Decentralized Service Delivery in Ethiopia

3.1 Overview of Decentralization and Service Delivery until 1991

Until 1991, Ethiopia has been a unitary state and deconcentrated and delegated forms of decentralization have characterized public service delivery. The country has been mainly characterized by centralization of power though there were some efforts at institutionalizing some form of decentralization. Under the Imperial Government, the country has been characterized by a centralized political-administrative system. In the era of the *Derg*, despite the regime's support for self- government and local autonomy, the system didn't take any meaningful measure to institute a devolved system of governance (Rasheed and Luke 1995, 74). Provision of service delivery at the local level has been the responsibility of central ministries, thus rendering local governments powerless and also inhibiting the development of local actors that could participate in local development.

Despite the existence of weredas as the lower tiers of government since the 1940s, the role of weredas in providing public services at the local level remained highly limited. Attempts at decentralization under the Imperial government and military rule popularly known as the *Derg*, remained insignificant owning to strict control of public services in a centralized manner. The experience under the Imperial government has been limited as stipulated in decree No. 1 enacted in 1942 that established provincial governments to act on behalf of the Emperor who had a final say on overall aspects of administration (Imperial Government of Ethiopia, Negarit Gazeta No. 6 of 1942, Article 1, Parts 7 & 31). At the beginning, provincial governors were assigned and acted under the supervision of the center. Later, they were brought under the Ministry of Interior as salaried civil servants and became agents of the central government *(ibid)*. In an attempt to respond to the pressure of modernization, the Emperor also enacted a decree in 1962 to allow for the establishment of pilot Sub-Provinces (*'awrajas'*) for self-administration. This attempt has also failed without any significant change due to lack of commitment by the Emperor to defend the policy and the reluctance and fear of the then parliament on the pretext that the decree could encourage political instability and secession (Meheret 1998, 8; Van-der Loop 2002, 13).

The main purpose of wereda administration at the time was enforcement of law and order and collection of taxes and only a few agencies like the police, finance and justice were fielded at wereda level. These services were centrally budgeted and controlled (Imperial Government, Negarit Gazeta No. 6 of 1942 Article 1, Part 31). All locally generated revenue was remitted to the central treasury. Under the military rule also, this limited role was maintained, until weredas were dissolved in 1987. Some additional roles were also assigned to weredas as a result of the Land Reform and Urban Land Proclamation, which established Peasant and Urban Dwellers Associations, following the Ethiopian Revolution of 1974. With these changes, weredas were given responsibility for implementing decisions related to the land reform, transmitting and enforcing rules and directives flowing from higher levels of administration, adjudicating minor litigations among community members and undertaking matters related to local development and service delivery (Tegegne and Kassahun 2004, 40-42).

Furthermore, both the jurisdictions and competence of local administrations have kept on changing from time to time particularly following regime changes. As indicated above, Decree No. 1 of 1942 created 12 *awrajas* and 60 *weredas*. But Decree No. 6 of 1946 changed sub-provinces (*awrajas)* to Provinces and *weredas* to sub-provinces and created *wereda* structures from below in place of the earlier *kebeles* by dividing the administration into three tiers (Imperial Government, Decree No. 6 of 1946). These tiers (province, *awrajas* and *weredas*) have served until *weredas* were abolished under *Derg* regime in 1987.

In 1987 the *Derg* established the Institute of Nationalities, which drafted a constitution that established five autonomous regions and 25 administrative regions with 354 sub-provinces *awrajas* thereby abolishing *weredas* as administrative tiers. Though the objective of granting autonomy under the *Derg* for the 5 regions (Tigray, Afar, Somali, Aseb and Gambella) was to respond to the demands of opposition groups through granting of self-rule, no significant progress was made in allowing the participation of the regions in the administration. Since the head of administration and some of the rank and files were assigned by the central government, the regions concerned were rather reduced to the strict control and supervision of the center. On matters of socio-economic development also, central planning has been a guiding principle in which local services were decided centrally. Local units are obliged to unconditionally comply with laws, directives and regulations and decisions of the center. Both physical and financial plans were approved from the center and required to follow standard reporting formats. Like the situation under the Imperial government, locally generated revenue should either be remitted to the central treasury or be endorsed by the council of state to be utilized locally. The minor changes made under military rule in regional and local administration is only change in names of provinces, and designation of local and regional officials.

Under both the Imperial government and military rule, decentralization efforts that aim to ensure empowerment and participation of citizens never existed. Neither officials were elected nor were they accountable to local people. Hence attempts at decentralization under both the Imperial and the Derg rules were made with the intention of only responding to the pressures from modernization and opposition groups with strict control of the center. The country remained under a centralized system of government with the objective of building strong centralist state in all aspects. Therefore, *weredas* have served as deconcentrated agents or field units of the central government and at times they functioned in the form of controlled delegation for convenience of centralized administration contrary to principles governing existence of local governments and adequate authority (Meheret 1998, 8-9; Tegegne and Kassahun 2004, 42). Furthermore, since the main structures for public service delivery were transferred from *weredas* to *awrajas* from 1987, only peasant and urban dwellers associations remained, which are neither mandated to play the role of weredas nor have the capacity to render required services to the local population.

3.2 Institutional Arrangements for Decentralized Service Delivery at Wereda Level

A decentralized governance system is a recent phenomenon, which is a significant departure from the history of the country in general. Since 1991, the country followed a new socio-economic and political direction with a policy that potentially allowed self-determination for the various nations, nationalities and peoples. The foundation for decentralized form of governance in the country has been laid down by the 1995 Ethiopian Federal Constitution, which established national regional states and defined the powers of the federal and regional governments. This became a framework for instituting a decentralized approach in governance and the prime responsibility for the delivery of basic services falls within the regional governments (Federal Democratic Republic of Ethiopia, Constitution 1995, Art. 50 & 52). At the same time, the country embarked on the task of economic adjustment and reconstruction through economic reforms (Hamdok 2003, 25). According to Befekadu (1994, 6), the reform was aimed at limiting the role of the state in the economy through privatization and focus on strategic and regulatory functions and to reduce the role of central government by shifting responsibilities to regional governments in particular.

Article 50(4) of the 1995 federal constitution states that each regional state can devolve adequate decision making authority and control over resources to lower levels of government in order to promote decentralization and bring government closer to the people. The constitution provided legal bases for wereda administration as important local government unit and required regional states to grant adequate power to the lowest units of government so that the latter serve as democratic organs of the government. This was aimed through empowerment of the communities at grass root level and by creating close interaction between the local administrative units and the people through direct participation of people in the administrative affairs of local governments. Empowerment at the grassroots is seen as a key to the improvement of service delivery. To implement these provisions at first stage, wereda administrations, which have been served as a deconcentrated unit of administration during the periods of the Imperial and Derg rules and also abolished from 1987, were reemerged from 1991 with representative institutions.

However, throughout the 1990s the initiative for decentralization has been limited to the regional level without any clear definition of the role of the lower tiers of government. Wereda*s* were initially empowered to undertake delivery of public services under the mandate of central, regional and zonal offices. It is only from 2001 onwards that Ethiopia began to adopt a decentralized form of local governance characterized by devolution. Devolution of power to the lower units of government *(wereda)* is also a recent phenomenon after almost 10 years of devolving authority to regions. During the period between 1991-2001, power of planning and implementing local services was based at regional and zonal levels while weredas were considered as field administrative agents or subordinate units of zonal administrations, with no authority to act as local autonomous entities. Under Zonal administration, weredas were given too much responsibility and functions but they lacked the necessary financial and resource capacity to undertake development at the local level (Befekadu 1994, 63). Thus, weredas could not exercise sufficient local autonomy and the performance of the weredas as effective units of government has been constrained by a number of inter-related factors. These include a number of factors such as tight control of *wereda* administrations and constant interference by zonal authorities, limited institutional and management capacity of wereda councils, inadequate administrative and personnel capacity, poor revenue base to carry out socioeconomic functions, and a high degree of dependence on regional states for financial allocation as well as limited space for political competition and participation of civil society at the wereda level (Meheret 1998). While regions are endowed with substantial amount of resources to match at least part of the devolved responsibilities, the process of decentralization at wereda level did not make much headway prior to 2001.This necessitated changes through devolution of power in financial and human resources that took place since 2001. In line with the federal constitution the second generation of decentralization started in four regional states (Oromia, Tigray, Amhara and South Nations and Nationalities) through legal and administrative measures undertaken in their respective revised constitutions since 2001.

Wereda/district decentralization has been initiated as one of the reform measures in the country underlining poverty reduction. Ethiopia's The Sustainable Development and Poverty Reduction Program (SDPRP) has components of governance and decentralization as its building blocks. In the document decentralization has been defined as one of the pillars of the Ethiopian poverty reduction strategy. It is stressed that the system of decentralization offers a framework for action and improved service delivery. In charging the regions with the responsibility of providing social services and carrying out poverty reduction programs, it is believed that decentralization brings about higher efficiency and better accountability in service delivery. It is also viewed as an effective way of bringing the decision-making process closer to the people, which enables the people to participate directly in their own development (MoFED 2002b, 39), Different sector programs such as education; health, water and road were adopted with focus on poverty reduction and sustainable development, deepening democratization, and good governance and empowerment. Based on the poverty reduction program, all sector programs have also adopted a system of decentralized service delivery through popular participation to facilitate access of public services to the population (MoFED 2002b).

To facilitate the delivery of public services various reforms were introduced for promoting effective governance both at the central and local levels and different institutional reform measures were taken through adoption of a National Capacity Building Program (NCBP). The program has been designed to build capacity at all levels of government. At the federal and regional levels capacity building offices were opened with the objective of building capacity at all levels. In the program, particular emphasis has been given to wereda decentralization as a means of empowering local communities, developing democratization and improving delivery of public services (Ministry of Capacity Building 2003).

With this and other motives, decentralization has been instituted at wereda level in different regions of the country since 2001. The Oromia National Regional State, which is one of the major regions of the country, defined the duties and responsibilities of the weredas in the region in its revised regional constitution of 2001. Weredas in the region were given the responsibility of planning, budgeting and implementation of public service delivery signified by expanded functions and mandates. In the constitution, wereda administrations have been given autonomy in expenditure prioritization when planning basic services. Weredas are empowered to deliver basic services such as agricultural extension, education, health, water supply, rural roads, etc., within their respective jurisdiction (Oromia National Regional State Revised Constitution 2001, Art.35-42). In accordance with this provision, different public sector offices have been instituted at the wereda level with the objective of making weredas the center of socio-economic development. It was also to provide a basis for meaningful participation by the people in local development programs. This was mainly designed to be implemented through deployment of different offices responsible for providing a range of services, including administrative and infrastructure services, and provision of primary education, primary health care, rural water supply, rural roads and agricultural extension. The focus given to these sectors and their delivery at the local level is due to their main role in realizing national development objectives.

With these provisions, regional states have recognized weredas and *kebeles* as legitimate units of local government administration with legally defined authority and functions and re-instituted weredas with a substantial devolved authority. Following the revision of the regional constitution, preliminary studies were conducted on institutional, administrative, personnel, fiscal and capacity building aspects of decentralization. Functional assignments were reorganized by transferring financial and administrative powers to weredas over revenue and expenditure authorities and personnel administration. Accordingly, weredas were restructured and reorganized with their own organizational structures and manpower and deployment of manpower has taken place from regions and zones since 2001. By 2002, a regional block grant has been introduced so that weredas can finance their expenditure needs. Different capacity building efforts were also made in view of the weak implementation capacities observed in the processes of wereda decentralization (Worku 2005, 29-35). In this process, weredas are considered as the basic unit and important lower level local institution and center of development because of their key role in prioritizing the provision of public services at the local level. They are also considered as a strategic unit of government for the implementation of the country's development strategies such as rural development, expansion of educational and health services, and sustainable development and poverty reduction.

4. Evaluation of Performances and Constraints

4.1 Performances of Selected Public Services

Despite some general improvements in public service delivery in the wereda, there is not much variation in overall performance between the period before and after decentralization. There is no commensurate progress among different public services in the wereda. The role of different actors and constraints encountered have also contributed to less than expected performance and variations among the performances of agencies engaged in public service delivery.

Performance in the education sector is better as compared to other public services during decentralization years. The major improvements in the sector are reduction in dropout rate and rate of repeaters and increase in participation of the community in school construction. When the periods before and after decentralization are compared, on average the number of schools increased from 20 to 28 (by 40%), with 65% increase in the number of sections from 154 to 254. Community involvement was also found to be greater in construction of schools and employing of teachers. Schools were directly constructed by the community in collaboration with other actors outside the wereda. The number of teachers also increased from 299 to 381, by 27%. Gross enrollment increased by a difference of 6,083 (64.3%) for girls and 4,918.8 (41.6%) for boys than prior to decentralization. The average number of non-dropouts was 14,581 for girls and 15,518 for boys, showing a difference of 6,114 (72.2%) and 4,958 (46.9%), respectively, than before decentralization. The number of non-repeaters also increased by a difference of 4,480 (54.4%) for girls and 3,048 (29.6%) for boys than before decentralization.

Seen against the standard used by the World Health Organization (WHO), which is also applied by the Ministry of Health, health service coverage by health infrastructures at the national level has shown an increasing trend from 50.71% to 72.1% in 1999/00 and 2004/05, respectively. In Oromia region also, a similar trend has been observed from 53.17% to 67.2% during the same periods. However, the coverage of health infrastructures in the wereda was from 48.5 percent to 49.2 percent during the periods. The wereda health center serves the whole population and administers the three health stations and three health posts in the wereda, which is below standard. Before decentralization, the coverage of health infrastructures in the wereda was on average 48.4 while the national and Oromia coverage was 54.5 percent and 52.5 percent, respectively.

After decentralization, the coverage became 50.6 percent while the national and Oromia coverage was 65.8 percent and 62.1 percent, respectively, which is still better than the wereda coverage before decentralization. The difference in health infrastructure coverage in the wereda between the periods before and after decentralization is only by 2.1 percent, which is registered after decentralization.

At current estimate of the wereda population and the standard, the existing health center and 3 health stations should each serve 1/5th of the population and the existing 3 health posts should each serve 1/7th of the population. But the health units are serving below standard due to population growth and lack of additional health infrastructure and scarcity of health professionals. In the case of health professionals also, the ratio of the wereda is the lowest, particularly after decentralization due to lack of medical doctors and resignation or transfer of five health assistants existing before decentralization, lack of replacement, and increase in the size of the population. After wereda decentralization, on average one health assistant serves 6,264 people in Oromia region while in the wereda the average is 1:8,139. In both health infrastructure coverage and health professionals, the wereda is below the regional coverage which implies that there are other weredas which are getting better services than the wereda. This also has implications for the efficiency of the wereda performance.

The performance of the wereda in immunization service has been on average below 40 percent both before and after decentralization. Despite the opening of a health office at the wereda and the opening of one additional health post, the performance after decentralization didn't show a significant improvement. The total number of people that received immunization service pertaining to maternal and child health care has on average reached 54,293, showing a difference of additional services for 9,417 people, which is greater by 3.5 percent than prior to decentralization. When this performance is compared with the planned target of services during the years of decentralization the performance is on average 37.5 percent.

In water supply and rural road sectors also, existing data indicate that the improvement is not that much significant. The water supply coverage for the wereda shows some improvements since 2004/05, but this improvement has not been attained due to wereda decentralization. Even though there are some inputs from the wereda communities in terms of labor and finance, the schemes constructed after decentralization were undertaken by the regional water bureau and Ethiopian Social Rehabilitation and Development Fund (ESRDF). The water supply in the wereda capital was constructed by the regional water Bureau and is still run under financial and technical assistance from the zonal water department and with no direct input from both the wereda water office and wereda administration. The seven rural water supply schemes that began providing services in the decentralization years were also constructed by the ESRDF, with labor and financial contribution from the respective community in each site.

Though the water supply coverage of the wereda has shown some improvement due to this contribution in the years of decentralization, the coverage is still 30%, which is the lowest compared to national and Oromia coverage. Furthermore, the performance of water supply activity by the wereda water office after decentralization is one of the lowest compared to other public services in the wereda. During the post-decentralization period, no water supply activity has been performed by the wereda office. All the existing schemes were constructed under institutions outside the wereda office. Even though the office is one of the new offices established following decentralization and has lots of constraints, so far nothing has been registered in terms of better performance in the field of water supply. Hence the contribution or benefits of decentralization to the wereda through this office is almost none.

Access to clean water supply has improved relatively due to construction of the water supply in the wereda capital and other small schemes in rural areas by other institutions outside the wereda office. However, the majority of the wereda population has no access to clean water. The above estimate of water coverage in the wereda shows that from the total population of the wereda, only 30.0 percent have access to clean water while the remaining use unprotected springs and rivers as sources. Compared to the national and regional coverage, the coverage of the wereda is also very low. Coverage at national level has increased from 34.13 percent in 2001/02 to 42.0 percent in 2004/05.During the same period, the coverage for Oromia region has also increased from 35.1 percent to 50.3 percent. In this comparison, though the wereda coverage has also shown similar improvements, it should have brought significant improvement if the office had increased the number of schemes and expanded existing schemes. As a result, the coverage of the wereda is expected to decrease with the increase in the size of the population and as the design period of existing schemes is nearing completion.

In the rural road sector, it was not possible to make comparisons of the state of affairs before and after decentralization owing to lack of data. There were no organized efforts in rural road construction and maintenance before decentralization. After the establishment of the rural roads office, and in view of its capacity and duration, its performance is relatively better compared to earlier times. This was made possible owing to activities of mobilizing and organizing the community and surveying the construction and maintenance of rural roads and bridges at a later stage. After decentralization, due to the establishment of the office at the *wereda* level, there are general improvements in organizing and mobilizing the community, which made possible labor contribution in rural road construction and maintenance.

Though traditionally people used to construct rural roads by contributing labor, this activity has been relatively better organized and operated in a planned manner with the establishment of the office under decentralization scheme. In this case, decentralization is creating a sense of partnership and ownership in local service delivery through close interaction between the office and the people who were encouraged to identify their needs. The undertaking is promising particularly in increasing the participation of the community. However, in this field also there are limitations in ensuring effective and quality performance due to lack of proper design and shortage of improved tools. Most of the roads constructed are poor in quality and their sustainability is already in danger.

When each of the public services is considered independently, there are some general improvements after decentralization on the basis of average performance. However, when the input of other actors outside the wereda institutions is considered with the wereda's own performance and the pace at which public service delivery has been performing before decentralization is considered, the overall performance is expected to be lower than what has been observed in the performance of the wereda in the selected public services. The performance of decentralization can also be influenced by different factors, which makes it difficult to conclude that decentralization is the only factor responsible for all performances. For example population growth affects the performance of education sector in terms of gross enrollment. In health service also, different variables such as prevalence rate of diseases, efficiency of professionals and availability and effectiveness of drugs and types of treatments given could determine changes in health service delivery before decentralization and after decentralization. Measuring the performance of decentralization is also difficult since there is no universally agreed upon measurement criteria. There are no clearly defined indicators against which its performance could be measured. There are also information constraints to fully assess the performance of decentralization as data collection and analysis are poorly developed not only at the wereda level but also at the regional and federal levels. At the same time decentralization is an ongoing process and it is difficult to get or collect all sorts of information and make an all-embracing and conclusive generalization. Lower performance also may be attributed to low efficiency of the wereda due to different constraints.

4.2 Constraints

There are still lots of constraints that undermine the efforts of the wereda administration in the post-decentralization period. These constraints revolve around weak coordination and participation particularly in terms of identifying local problems and prioritizing and attaining local needs. Constraints in budget and manpower are also factors significantly affecting the delivery of public services in the wereda. The planning processes in the wereda indicate weak coordination and participation in identifying problems and prioritizing public services. Sector office plans and kebele plans are sent independently to the wereda executive committee, which discuses and recommends the annual plan and budget for approval by the council. Although, public services require government budget and community input in terms of labor and finance, all public services are related with sectoral issues and there is no reason to treat the plan of kebele and sectors independently. The kebele administration does not have sector offices, as in the case of the wereda, to implement plans for each sector. Lack of coordination and integration in sector plans and kebele plans has also its own impact on involving the community in prioritizing local services according to local needs. Each office prepares its annual plan without assessment of required activities in consultation with the target groups and submits for approval to the wereda administration

In involving the community, even though some consultations with the community particularly at school levels take place, the consultation is not aimed at identifying the problems faced by communities and prioritizing them. Measures to improve the involvement of the community members in planning and budgeting public services are not given much attention. Participation of the community in problem identification and prioritization is rarely witnessed and the role of the community is limited to provision of labor and materials during implementation.

Coordination both at the wereda offices and kebele level is weak. Even though the Office for Finance and Economic Development was established to play the role of coordinating the planning and budgeting process, it is staffed by non-qualified experts. At the same time, although the kebele administration has been established as a mechanism to reach people at the grassroots level, there is no clearly institutionalized structure for enhancing the coordination and participation of the local communities in this process. On one hand, the structure of kebele administrations is not staffed by fulltime personnel and the members of the kebele cabinet are self-employed receiving a token monthly allowance of between 50 and 150 Birr. Secondly, though kebeles are organized under *gotes* and teams, almost all of them are not functional and effective. The role of kebele administration itself is limited to community mobilization and reporting of such activities as required from wereda administration. Hence, there is a problem in addressing the priority needs of the community. All the public services are normally decided and provided by civil servants who feel accountability to their respective institutions and to the wereda administration rather than to the public. The decision-making process is still hierarchical in all the planning and budgeting processes. Community input or its role in planning and budgeting is very low or non-existent except making labor and financial contributions. Therefore, the role of the people in the wereda in the processes of decision-making and provision of public services thereof is minimal at best. Efforts at studying local conditions and flexibility of needs and considerations for local needs and priorities are constrained by lack of participation and lack of capacity, among others. Service delivery role in the wereda is highly concentrated at the wereda level with limited role given to lower administrative tier - the kebeles and the community at large.

In terms of budget also, there is a great mismatch between its expenditure obligation and the financial resources it actually receives in the form of block grant and use of own revenue. Wereda's own revenue and regional block grant are still lagging behind the wereda expenditure requirement for provision of public services. In the periods before decentralization from 1997/98 to 2000/01, locally generated revenue on average amounted to 2.0 million Birr while after decentralization there was a slight increase amounting to 2.1 million Birr. From this it is possible to observe that the amount of revenue generated after decentralization didn't show much increase compared with the amount of revenue collected before decentralization and also when compared with the expenditure need of the wereda after decentralization. The amount of contribution of locally generated revenue to the wereda budget has been on average 43 percent and 29 percent before decentralization and after decentralization, respectively. During the post-decentralization period the maximum contribution of local revenue to the wereda budget has been 33 percent, which has been the least contribution in the years before decentralization.

The main reasons for such limited revenue base could be explained by different factors. Since the wereda is lacking significant revenue originating from urban centers, agricultural income and land use fees account for a major portion of revenue, which is not significant as such. The other reason for the low revenue is lack of awareness, lack of interest to pay, fluctuations of climatic conditions impoverishing households. However, the basic reason that explains low level of revenue in the wereda is absence of appropriate assessment in local potentials and inadequacies associated with collection. The annual collection plan is prepared and sent by the regional authorities and the role of the wereda has been limited in meeting the target. There is no assessment of revenue potential of the wereda and the difference among different payers.

Notwithstanding this, however, the expenditure need of the wereda has increased annually since decentralization. The wereda budget has increased from 4.0 million Birr in 1997/98 to 8.8 million Birr in 2005/06. With such an increase, the major portion of the wereda budget has been financed by the regional block grant. Despite the growing need for local development and public services, the wereda remained dependent on regionally transferred grants. The budget transfer to the wereda before decentralization on average amounted to 57 percent from 1997/98 to 2001/02 while the share of block grant to the wereda budget has been between 67 percent and 82 percent during decentralization years. After decentralization, the wereda has been dependent on the regional block grant for its expenditure and the dependency has shown an increasing trend from year to year. This was expected to show a decreasing trend after decentralization.

Besides, the main reason for low-level services in the wereda also could be explained by the wereda budget allocation system that lacks equity in terms of fairness. There are great variations in the budget allocated for the sectors. Education has the biggest share with more than 50 percent of the total budget whereas health, water and road sectors receive the lowest share. Health sector has got less than 10 percent of the total budget varying between 2.5 percent and 7.9 percent. Water supply and rural roads have got a similar allocation varying between 0.1 percent and 0.4 percent of the total annual budget. Even in education where there is a relatively better allocation, the sector faces budget constraints for operation cost. The schools receive only some materials in kind from the wereda education office and they never get budget for operation cost in the form of cash. Consequently, at Primary level (1-8th) between 2002/03 and 2005/06, the per capita was within the range of 1 Birr and 30 cents to 77 cents, which is extremely low. Similarly, per capita for 9th and 10th grades was also low but relatively better when compared with what has been allocated at Primary level. In health also, the total budget allocated for health services in the wereda is very low contrary to the fact that health service is in the top list of community priorities. The amount of budget allocated for operation cost of the health sector is very low despite the scarcity of medical facilities, medicine and humanpower at all health units. The average per capita for health from 2002/03 to 2004/05 in the wereda is 4 Birr and 20 cents, which is by far below both the national and the regional average. The per capita at the national and Oromia region was 13.8 and 5.7, respectively, during the same period.

In water supply and rural road sector, the allocation system didn't take into consideration the priority needs of the community. The amount allocated didn't show significant changes over the years. Budget allocated for both sectors in each of the years of decentralization remained below 1% of the total *wereda* budget. This small amount is also paid for salary of the staff and what is allocated as operation cost does not exceed costs for minor stationary items.

Furthermore, the trend in expenditure has shown an increase in salary expenditure than operation costs. Hence the bulk of the wereda budget goes for payment of salaries of civil servants in the wereda. Salary expenditure is between 83.5 percent and 92.2 percent while operation costs have been between 7.8 percent and 16 percent in the years of decentralization. After decentralization, increase in the number of schools and teachers and the opening of additional new offices and assignment of new employees for these offices are among the reasons for increase in salary expenditure in the wereda.

On the other hand, despite the proximity of the wereda to the zonal capital and its location on the main road, the wereda is facing humanpower problem, inhibiting efficient delivery of public services. This is mainly because of lack of clearly institutionalized structure and scarcity of humanpower both in quantity and quality. The existing structure for education and health offices in the wereda does not indicate all required posts. There is no clearly defined structure for required number of teachers at both primary and secondary schools, and at health stations and health posts. In terms of availability of humanpower, from the total number of

847 vacant posts in the selected public service agencies of the wereda, only 593 have been filled. In terms of quality of humanpower, too, problems are encountered; only 18 are degree holders, 219 are have diplomas and the remaining are 12+1 and below. Most of the unfilled vacant posts are those that are needed to provide required public service in the wereda, particularly at frontline agencies such as teachers and health assistants. Due to lack of required number of teachers with required training at first and second cycles and secondary level, teachers whose educational level does not satisfy the educational requirement for their present assignment are providing education services. According to the requirement, graduates of Teacher Training Institutes (TTI) are eligible to teach up to first cycle and diploma graduates are eligible to teach up to 8th grade while $9-10^{th}$ should be only undertaken by first-degree holders. In the case of the wereda, TTI graduates teach up to 8th grade and diploma graduates teach up to 10th grade. As indicated in table 1, the majority of the teachers in the wereda are from TTIs while the majority of the schools are up to 8th grade, which require diploma graduates particularly for $5^{th}-8^{th}$ grades. Furthermore community-employed teachers whose educational level is between 10th grade and TTI level also fill most of the vacant posts. The number of teachers employed by communities is increasing each year and on average 104 of the teachers who teach from $1-8^{th}$ grade are community-employed teachers. This number has reached 148 in 2005/06 academic year. From the total of 41 teachers teaching in 9th and 10th grades, also 25 of them are diploma holders.

Similarly, one of the basic problems in health service delivery, particularly at health stations and health posts, is lack of structures to assign required personnel. There is no structure also for health extension workers. Hence, there is critical humanpower shortage at health stations and health posts. One of the determinants of health service is trained humanpower in the field. According to current statistics in the wereda, the existing health professionals and facilities (health center, health station and health post) do not match each other. Only the health center in the wereda town is relatively capable of providing daily regular services with better humanpower and facilities. At each of the health stations and health posts serving communities, there is only one health assistant and one cleaner or casher. Since one health assistant runs a health unit, he/she is incapable of providing required services regularly due to annual leave or personal problems. In case of total absence due to resignation or other reasons, provision of health services is interrupted until replacement is found. Besides, no study has been conducted regarding the humanpower requirement at the health station and health post levels and there is no clear structure to fill required humanpower gaps. Even though there is a similar humanpower problem in water and rural roads sectors, the most critical problem is related with effective utilization of the existing humanpower. The existing humanpower at these offices is not utilized efficiently mainly due to budget constraints compared to other offices.

The wereda is also constrained by other institutional issues related with regulations made at regional and zonal levels. One of the powers given to weredas is to administer their humanpower in matters related with personnel management. Devolution of power is meant to include the power to hire, fire and promote employees. Proclamation No.61/94 of the Oromia National Regional State also gives equal power and responsibility to all public offices in the region in personnel management. According to the proclamation, all offices in the region are given power to hire, fire, and promote in line with provisions of the proclamation. But weredas are restricted by other internal regulations not to employ without prior approval of the regional Civil Service Office. This prevents filling vacant posts without the prior agreement of the Regional Civil Service Bureau. Any vacant post should be agreed to and allowed by the regional Civil Service Bureau before making transfers, employment, and promotion. Although the reason behind the restriction is to balance the flow of humanpower among weredas and to control employment in terms of priority needs due to budget limitations, the mechanism has imposed restrictions on the exercise of the power given to the wereda.

5. Summary and Conclusion

Given the theoretical assumptions about decentralization, there is sufficient reason to believe that service delivery by local authorities is more efficient, flexible and responsive to local needs and conditions than delivery by federal, regional and zonal bodies. Despite these theoretical assumptions and the pertinent constitutional provisions, both at federal and regional levels, to effectively institute a decentralized system, the initiative is still characterized by low efficiency and less responsiveness as seen from the findings. Though some improvements were witnessed after decentralization, it is difficult to conclude that this has brought significant changes in the major sectors of public service delivery. When overall performance is measured by including the inputs of the regional, zonal and other actors, some improvements have been witnessed. However, when the inputs of actors outside the wereda institutions and other contributing factors or variables are disregarded, performance in the post-decentralization years in the wereda has not been impressive. With the exception of opening up of some new offices that did not exist before decentralization and the introduction of exercise of power over expenditure management and some minor differences in performances, it is possible to conclude that the performance of the wereda has been impeded by different constraints which obliged the wereda to act almost in the same manner as before decentralization. This leads one to conclude that the wereda is not efficient in public service delivery as envisaged to be during the post-decentralization years.

Different constraints are responsible for the drawbacks. Financial and humanpower constraints and problems of coordination and participation have basically contributed to low performance of the wereda. Though the wereda was given autonomy in planning, administering, and managing public services, it has been restricted in terms of fully exercising its devolved powers particularly in personnel administration due to the actions of the regional and zonal bodies as well as the local challenges facing the wereda. Inconsistency of rules and regulations originating from regional and zonal bodies as regards planning and personnel administration are some of the impediments that inhibited the exercise of devolved power. For example, local revenue collection is based on regional plan whereas employment, transfer and promotion of staff are controlled both by regional and zonal bodies. These are compounded by budgetary and humanpower constraints. Therefore, it is difficult to make the wereda accountable for its low performance in the absence of full autonomy in exercising its powers.

On the part of the wereda also there is no significant effort in adjusting priorities according to local needs. Identification of priority needs and allocation of commensurate budget to address these needs is what has not been taken seriously on the part of the wereda. Mechanisms and modalities for delivering public services are still determined by the sector offices culminating in approval of the cabinet without input from the community, which makes accountability relationship weak. As far as there are no commonly designed and agreed on plans, it is difficult to make service providers accountable. These are particularly manifested in planning and budgeting processes. Annual discussion on budget preparation and approval excludes concerned experts and is decided in council and cabinet meetings alone. As a result, the budget allocated for public services is not properly defended by experts from the concerned offices before cabinet decision is made. This has contributed to lack of focus on some important public services entailing insignificant budget allocation to services like health and water supply. Existing effort underlines matching available finance with national and regional priorities without lending attention to assessment of local needs. It is worthy to note, however, that planning and budgeting is more than matching existing resources with national and regional priorities. The wereda has also limited its annual plan for collection of local revenue to fit to plans made at regional level without trying to go beyond set targets. This has limited the capacity of the wereda in delivering public services at the required level and made it increasingly dependent on block grants. This is contrary to the theoretical assumptions of decentralization and the views held locally that the wereda is among the best performing ones in Arsi Zone.

This challenge offers important opportunities for enhanced service delivery through increased public sector efficiency. An adequate, efficient, effective and responsive system is a prerequisite to provide quantity and quality services in meeting basic human needs. In this case as indicated above, there are still a number of prerequisites to be fulfilled to provide services with increased efficiency and responsiveness under the decentralization initiative. Without putting in place these prerequisites and addressing those factors contributing to poor performance, a policy of decentralization alone does not produce intended results.

References

Bailey, Stephan J. 1999. *Local government economics, principles and practice.* London: Macmillan.

Barlow, I.M. 1981. *Spatial dimensions of urban government.* New York: Research Studies Press.

Befekadu Degefe. 1994. The legal framework for fiscal decentralization in Ethiopia. In *Fiscal decentralization in Ethiopia*, edited by Eshetu Chole. Addis Ababa: Addis Ababa University Press.

Bhatta, Gambhir. 1998. *Governance innovations in the Asian-Pacific Region: Trends, causes and issues.* USA: Ashgate.

Bulti Terffassa. 1994. The role of fiscal decentralization in promoting participatory development in Ethiopia. In *Fiscal decentralization in Ethiopia,* edited by Eshetu Chole. Addis Ababa: Addis Ababa University printing Press.

Central Statistical Authority (CSA). 2002/03, 2003/04, 2004/05 & 2005/06. *Statistical Abstract.* Addis Ababa: CSA.

_____. 2004. *Welfare monitoring survey: Analytical report.* Addis Ababa: CSA.

Chikulo, B.C. 1998. Decentralization and the role of the state in the future. In *Governance and human development in Southern Africa*, edited by Ibbo Mandoza. Harare: SAPES TRUST.

Doornbos, Martin. 2000. *Institutionalizing development policies and resource strategies in Eastern Africa and India.* London: Institute of Social Studies.

Dunleavy, Patrick, and Brendan O'leary. 1981. *Theories of the State: The politics of liberal democracy.* London: Macmillan.

Elcak, Howard. 1994. *Local government: Policy and management in local Authorities.* London: Rutledge.

Federal Democratic Republic of Ethiopia (FDRE). 1995. *Constitution of the Federal Democratic Republic of Ethiopia.* Addis Ababa: FDRE.

Gant, George F. 1979. *Development administration: Concepts, goals and methods.* London: University of Wisconsin Press.

Goss, Sue. 2001. *Making local governance work: Networks, relationships and the management of change.* New York: Palgrave.

Hailu Belay. 2003. *The current decentralization in Ethiopia: Prospects and challenges.* RLDS Working Paper No.14. Regional and Local Development Studies, Addis Ababa University. Addis Ababa.

Hamdok, Abdalla. 2003. Governance and policy in Africa: Recent experiences. In *Reforming Africa's institutions: Ownership, incentives, and capabilities,* edited by Steve Kayizze-Mugerwa. New York: United Nations University Press.

Imperial Government of Ethiopia. 1942. Decree No.1 of 1942, Negarit Gazeta No. 6 1942, Addis Ababa.

_____. 1942. Decree No.6 of 1946, Negarit Gazeta 1946, Addis Ababa.

Kayizze-Mugerwa, Steve, ed. 2003. *Reforming Africa's institutions: Ownership, incentives, and capabilities.* New York: United Nations University Press.

Kibre Moges. 1994. The conceptual framework for fiscal decentralization. In *Fiscal decentralization in Ethiopia,* edited by Eshetu Chole. Addis Ababa: Addis Ababa University Press.

Martinussen, John. 1997. *Society, state and market: A guide to competing theories of development.* London: Zed.

Meheret Ayenew. 1998. *Some preliminary observations on institutional and administrative gaps in Ethiopia's decentralization processes.* Working Paper No.1, Regional and Local Development Studies (RLDS). Addis Ababa University, Addis Ababa.

Ministry of Capacity Building (MoCB). 2003. Public sector capacity building program. MoCB, Addis Ababa.

Ministry of Finance and Economic Development (MoFED). 2002a. Poverty profile of Ethiopia. MoFED, Addis Ababa.

_____. 2002b. *Ethiopia: Sustainable development and poverty reduction program.* Addis Ababa: MoFED.

Ministry of Health. 2002/03, 2003/04, 2004/05. *Health and health related indicators.* Addis Ababa: MoH.

Ministry of Water Resources. 2005. *Annual report.* Addis Ababa.

Munday, Stephen C.R. 1996. *Current developments in economics.* London: Macmillan.

Olowu, Dele. 2000. Metropolitan governance in developing countries. *Regional development studies*, Vol. 6. United Nations Centre for Regional Development, NAGOYA, Japan.

Oromia Civil Service Bureau. 2004. Wereda organizational structure. Finfinne.

Oromia National Regional State. 1994. Proclamation No.61/94,1994. Finfinne.

_____. 2001. Oromia Regional State Revised Constitution No.46/2001. Magalata Oromia, No.5, 2000, Finfinne.

Osborne, David, and Ted Gaebler. 1992. *Reinventing government.* New Delhi: Prentice-Hall of India.

Rasheed, Sadig, and David Fashole Luke. 1995. *Development management in Africa.* USA: West View.

Senboja, Joseph, and Ole Therkidsen. 1995. *Service provision under stress in East Africa.* Copenhagen: Center for Development Research.

Streeten, Paul Patrick. 1995. *Thinking about development.* New York: Cambridge University Press.

Tegegne Gebre-Egziabher and Asfaw Kumssa. 2002. Institutional setting for Local level development. *Regional development studies*, Vo.18. NAGOYA, Japan: United Nations Center for Regional Development.

Tegegne Gebre-Egziabher and Kassahun Berhanu. 2004. The role of Decentralized governance in building local institutions, diffusing ethnic conflicts, and alleviating poverty in Ethiopia. *Regional development dialogue,* Vo.25, No.1. NAGOYA, Japan: United Nations Center for Regional Development.

Turner, Mark, and David Hulme. 1997. Governance, administration and development: Making the state work. London: Macmillan.

UNDP. 2000. The UNDP role in decentralization and local governance. Evaluation Officer, New York.

_____. 2005. Human Development Report. New York: UNDP.

UN-HABITAT. 2002. Local democracy and decentralization in East and Southern Africa. Nairobi.

Van der Loop, Theo, ed. 2002. Local democracy and decentralization. In *Ethiopia, Regional and local development studies* (RLDS). Addis Ababa: Addis Ababa University and United Nations Human Settlements Programs.

Worku Yehualashet. 2005. District level decentralization in Ethiopia: Expenditure assignments and fiscal transfer. In *Issues and challenges in local and regional development*, edited by Tegegne Gebre Egziabher and Meine Pieter Van Dijk. Addis Ababa.

World Bank. 1997. *Annual Report 1997*. Washington, D.C.: Oxford University Press.

_____. 199/2000. *World development report: Entering the 21st century.* Washington, D.C.: Oxford University Press.

_____. 2000. *Annual report.* Washington, D.C.: Oxford University Press.

_____. 2004. *World development report: Making services work for Poor people.* Washington, D.C.: Oxford University Press.

IV

Decentralization and Education Service Delivery: The Case of Moretenna Jirru and Bereh Aleltu Weredas in North Shoa[*]

Tesfaye Tadesse

1. Introduction

Since 1991, Ethiopia has been experimenting with the policy of regionalization. This is aimed at devolving governmental power from the center to the regions. Regions are given a considerable degree of internal self-rule, including the authority to raise local revenue and administer their own budgets and development plans. Each Region consists of Zonal, Wereda and Kebele tiers of administration to which it transferred responsibilities and resources to promote decentralized governance.

Tegegne and Kassahun (2004) noted that the main objectives of Ethiopian decentralization policy are to enable the different ethnic groups to develop their culture and language, manage socio-economic development in their respective areas, exercise self-rule and bring about an equitable share of national resources.

Sustainable Development and Poverty Reduction Program annual Progress report of the year 2003 claims that weredas have been given greater economic and political power to implement development plans based on locally determined priorities, consistent with national sustainable development and poverty reduction program goals. It further states that district cabinets have been formed with functional representation from key public bodies organized to discharge public service delivery responsibilities. Further the Public Sector Capacity Building Program action plan (PSCAP 2003/04/2007/08) of the Amhara National Regional State underlines that the Amhara Regional state has taken measures to enable the community at grassroots level to exercise active participation in decision making on issues that affect their lives. The action plan acknowledges that the regional constitution bestowed Weredas with powers to exercise

---

[*] This chapter is based on the author's MA Thesis submitted to the Institute of Regional and Local Development Studies, Addis Ababa University, 2006.

authorities over their own affairs. The power to make decisions and functions of delivering services have greatly been devolved. In line with the above and as part of the overall decentralization process in Ethiopia, decentralization of educational management has been officially adopted through the 2002 Education and Training Policy of Ethiopia to create the necessary condition to expand, enrich and improve the relevance, quality, accessibility and equity of education and training. The literature on developing countries show that financial, human and physical resource constraints have inhibited the successful implementation of decentralization in nearly all developing countries (Rondinelli, Nellis and Cheema 1983). Studies in Kenya, the Sudan, and Tanzania show the crucial effects of shortages of trained manpower on the success of decentralization in those countries (Rondinelli, Nellis and Cheema 1983). Leadership and management training courses for local officials were found inadequate. The shortage of skilled staff at local level has been an equally important factor in the implementation of decentralization in Asia. Many programs are plagued with a chronic lack of trained technicians and managers.

The inadequacy of financial resources and the inability to allocate and expand them effectively were noted in evaluations of decentralization in nearly every developing country. The lack of independent sources of revenue weakened the organization's ability to carry out their decentralized tasks in India (Seminar on Effective Decentralization 2001). Shortage in skilled   personnel   and   financial   resources   have   also   undermined decentralization in Latin America. Because they lack financial resources, local governments have difficulty covering their basic operating expenses, training their personnel, purchasing equipment, making organizational improvements, obtaining technical assistance and expanding the range and quality of public service (Rondinelli Nellis and Cheema 1983).

In the light of the empirical evidences of developing countries from Africa, Latin America and Asia to carry out decentralization, the study would examine the availability of decision making power, the existence of skilled manpower, institutions that are endowed with the requirements for best performing their functions, the different local associations created (Kebele Education and Training Board and Parent Teacher Associations), their level of performance and limitations, and finally availability of adequate finance to carry out wereda and kebele level decentralized education service.

The general objective of the study is to examine the performance of dcentralized education service in Moretenna Jirru and Bereh Aleltu Weredas in Amhara and Oromia Regions by concentrating on variables such as power devolution, institution building, community participation and availability of adequate budget. To this effect the study focuses on the following specific objectives.

- Identify the key educational functions assigned to the concerned weredas and the corresponding decision making discretion exercised;

- Identify and analyze the institutions established and assess their level of performance;

- Examine the adequacy of budget allocation for education service in the weredas;

- Identify the level of community involvement to promote the service through participatory approach;

- Identify constraints, challenges, problems and achievements.

A case study of two Weredas, namely, Moretenna Jirru Wereda in Amhara Regional State and Bereh Aleltu in Oromia Regional State in North Shoa was undertaken.

The wereda level administration is the focal point for this study because of the strategic place it occupies with regard to its relative closeness to the grassroots communities and its being a viable unit of government for meaningful socio-economic development at the local level.

Each of the case study weredas was studied in its own right. Generalizations and observations drawn from the case studies are expected to be relevant to others since education service has a lot in common in most parts of the country. Primary data are collected using qualitative methods such as interviews of key informants, focus group discussions and field observation. The study population in both of the weredas includes elected representatives, political appointees, civil servants and community members.

In addition field observation of schools of different cycles was also made. Furthermore, official statistical sources, books, journals, internet sources and other publications have been consulted.

2. Conceptual Framework

Development theories of the 1950s and 1960s reflect the view that the central government alone had the capacity to provide public services and bring about development.

However, the economic crisis of the 1970's and the failure of the model to generate growth and reduce poverty, led more and more governments to initiate experiments in democratization and decentralization (Piriou 1998).

Decentralization can be defined as, "the transfer of planning, decision-making, or administrative authority from the central government to its field organizations, local administrative units, semi - autonomous local government or non-governmental organizations (Rondinelli Nellis and Cheema 1983). Decentralization is transferring authority and responsibility from the central government to field units or agencies, corporations, non-government and semi-autonomous public authorities, etc., to plan, manage, raise and allocate resources.

Rondinelli Nellis and Cheema's (1981) classification of the types of decentralization consists of deconcentration, devolution, and delegation.

The rationales for decentralization include the following. It is considered that decentralization allows tailored plans addressing the local and regional problems and needs; it helps to overcome delays and dysfunctions of a centralized bureaucracy; leads to more flexible, innovative and creative administration at the regional and district levels, bring government nearer to the people by facilitating both information exchange and accountability of authorities to citizens; and allows the representation and participation of various political, ethnic, and religious groups in national policy issues thereby fostering equitable resource allocation. Rondinelli says that decentralized governments serve as a training ground for local representatives to develop the skills and experience required to act on their own administrative capacity in managing their affairs and avoid inefficiency, increase the number of public goods and services. Decentralization is equally expected to help in achieving goals pertaining to poverty reduction, sustainable livelihoods, environmental protection and gender equality.

Decentralization and Service Delivery

Service delivery basically refers to the systematic arrangement of activities in service giving institutions with the objective of fulfilling the needs and expectations of service users and other stakeholders with the optimum use of resources. From this point of view the classic argument in favor of decentralization is that it increases the efficiency and responsiveness of government, locally elected leaders know their constituents better than authorities at the national level and so should be well positioned to provide the public services local residents want and need. This is based on the assumption that physical proximity makes it easier for citizens to hold local officials accountable for their performance.

Rondinelli, Nellis and Cheama (1983) argue that decentralization will improve governments' responsiveness to the public and increase the quantity and quality of services it provides. Many functions that are currently the responsibility of central ministries or agencies are performed poorly because of the difficulty of extending central services to local communities. Programs are decentralized with the expectation that delays will be reduced and indifference to satisfying the needs of the clientele are overcome.

The World Bank (1996) underlines that when decentralization is accompanied by local elections, government responsiveness increases markedly, improving the quantity, speed and quality of service delivery. The Banks states that local communities possess significant latent capacity which was earlier suppressed by centralized rule, for planning and implementing local micro projects. They can often deliver services more efficiently than conventional bureaucracies.

UNESCO has generally favored decentralization as one means of incorporating managerial groups in public decision making and improving the quality of services they receive (Winkler 1989). The action takes forms ranging from elected school boards in Chicago to school clusters in Cambodia to vouchers in Chile (Friske 1996). To show the importance of decentralization to service delivery Winkler (1989) argues that decentralization at the local level is more commonly undertaken as a means of democratization and increasing citizen participation and as a means of stimulating large financial contributions by the community.

3. Wereda Authorities and Responsibilities for Decentralized Education Management

The constitution of the Federal Democratic Republic of Ethiopia does not make a clear reference to the wereda administrative structures. But Article 50 provides that adequate power shall be granted to the lowest units of government to enable the people to participate directly in the administration of such units. On the other hand, Proclamation No. 59/2001n the revised constitution of the Amhara National Region State and Proclamation No. 46 (2001), and Proclamation of the Oromia region specify that the wereda administration shall comprise principal organs of power, namely, the wereda council. The main constitutional powers and duties of the wereda council and its executives are:

- Preparing and approving the annual wereda development plans and budgets and monitoring their implementation;

- Setting certain tax rates and collecting local taxes and levies (principally land use tax, agricultural income tax, sales taxes, and user fees.);

- Administering the fiscal resource available to the wereda;

- Constructing and maintaining low grade rural tracks, water points, and wereda level administrative infrastructure;

- Administering primary schools and health institutions;

- Managing agricultural development activities, and protecting natural resources.

A guideline for the Ministry of Education elaborates the planning responsibilities of a wereda education office. This includes planning the implementation of universal basic education, making projection on involvement, resources and preparing annual budget and carrying out audit. With regard to human resource management one finds that the wereda has the right and responsibility to recruit, assign transfer, promote and handle disciplinary cases. The above being the most important one, other activities such as project management, civil work, and procurement management responsibilities are devolved to the wereda level education. Pedagogical functions at the wereda level include implementation of primary and secondary school curriculum, distribution of instructional materials, establishing school clusters, carrying out adult education and community skills training programs and working towards ensuring that the quality of education complies with the approved standard.

The above being the general duties and responsibilities devolved to the wereda level of administration, the following section examines the extent to which these are responsibilities are exercised in Moretenna Jirru and Bereh Aleltu weredas. The assessment is made in terms of four variables, namely, institutional and resource capacity, school personnel, community participation and budget.

3.1. Institutional and Human Resource Capacity

Decentralization requires technical skills and organizational capability, which are scarce at the local level. The development of this capacity is an expensive and time consuming task that many of the developing countries cannot afford.

The Wereda Education Office in Moretenna Jirru was reported to have had a problem in durable leadership since those who were posted were continually resigning. According to most informants, this situation has hampered the service the office could have rendered. This was ascribed to the difficult working and living conditions in the wereda. Currently, the head of the Education Office is a diploma graduate with quite significant number of years of teaching experience. According to responses obtained from the office and other related sources, it was particularly difficult to get the professionals as per the requirements of the Education Office. This problem is not unique to this office alone. Other offices too face the same problem. The working environment, at least with regards to provision of adequate facilities, is unattractive. There is no adequate office space for all of the professionals and facilities such as tables, chairs and others are lacking. Apart from the shortage skilled human resource, school directors (e.g., Mangudo Director), point out the inefficiency of the service at the Wereda Education Office, as manifested long delays of responses to requests from schools.

Although these problems are generally shared by others, too, the Wereda Education Office in Bereh Aleltu reported that it does not face major human resource problems and that the qualification profile of staff is closer to the requirements of the administration. The office facilities are reported to be adequate. This could be due to the fact that the wereda is closer to Addis Ababa and is situated along the main transportation route to the capital.

3.2 Kebele Education and Training Board (KETB) and Parent/ Teacher Association (PTA)

These organizations were established to administer and lead school affairs. It is evident that institution building is very critical to foster development. Many capacity building programs consider institution building as a major component of their activity. In both Moretenna Jirru and Bereh Aleltu, KETB is claimed to be the next highest level of school administration. Composed of a minimum of seven members KETB includes a representative of a 'Kebele' administration as chairperson, the school headmaster as member and secretary, three representatives of the PTA, a teacher from the local teachers association and a member of a youth association. It is not hard to observe that KETB members are largely composed of members who are appointed on political consideration such as loyalty rather than representation of the community. The chairperson of KETB is the chairman of a kebele administration. If decentralization is about bringing decision making closer to the people with the intention of enhancing access to services, why is there a need to give the leadership to political nominees when the community can do it on an election basis. Duties and responsibilities of KETB's cover wide and diversified areas of responsibilities. But without any significant distinction between both of the weredas, interviews conducted with different education officials show that the education and experience of members is by far inferior to the overall responsibilities they are in charge of. Some of the members do not even recognize their duties and responsibilities. In addition, there are also problems of commitment. In general, KETB has more to do with control than being accountable to the community.

In both weredas, concerns expressed at different levels show that PTAs are relatively more fruitful in the effort to promote educational development. PTAs are composed of parents and teachers who are direct beneficiaries of a school. Gaynor (1998) notes that locally determined incentives seem to improve performance. But unfortunately this fact is not recognized or is ignored by those who are behind the idea of KETB. Evidence from El Salvado, Mexico, Nepal and Pakistan suggests that increase in school autonomy can lead to better teacher attendance and motivation. The World Bank underlines that the future style of management in the education system should be less encumbered by administrative and legislative rules, and it should grant more real independence for making decisions and more freedom for personal initiative at lower levels of the system.

3.3 School Personnel

In the case of Bereh Aleltu the number of teachers below the diploma level qualification are estimated to be 40%. In addition ,80% of the directors have a qualification that does not comply with the minimum requirement. Education officials admitted that this situation has negatively impacted on the service. The situation in Moretenna Jirru is also similar. For example, in the only one high school that exists, more than twenty teachers have qualification below the required level. This problem is further aggravated by shortage of teachers. The number of supervisors in both weredas is very much below what the activity requires. They are forced to cover long distances on foot with no transport allowance. Teachers strongly complain about their working condition. Among the problems one can cite pays, housing, and classrooms. There was no significant sensitization and consensus building effort made to integrate teachers in the process of educational decentralization. If decentralization is about improving the service delivery by bringing the decision making power closer to the grassroots level, one should witness efforts to empower the beneficiaries of decentralization. But this is not the case. People do not feel they are empowered or are not even aware of the trend. Rondinelli, Nellis and Cheama (1983) argue that genuine decentralization has to be institutionalized. They note that it must be equipped with trained and skilled personnel capable of coordinating and integrating their organizations. But in general the above is not generally true in both study weredas. Gaynor (1998) argues that the success of any decentralization of teachers management depends crucially on the cooperation of the teachers themselves. But this is not the case to say the least. It is really difficult to bring improved service delivery given the existing situation in both weredas.

Over all, it appears that in both Moretenna Jirru and Bereh Aleltu Weredas, education management up to the level of first cycle secondary school is devolved to the wereda level. Among the major functions one can site as an example teacher recruitment, school construction, upgrading of schools and budget allocation. With regard to the budget, major decisions about allocation on a sectoral basis is undertaken by the wereda council. The rest of the decisions are left to the discretion of a few individuals who are reported to be party members working in the wereda executive council and the wereda education office. Others such as the community, school personnel, Kebele Education and Training Board and Parent/Teacher Association come into the picture only during implementation. Their role in decision making is minimal. If the whole issue of decentralization is to bring the administration closer to the people and facilitate the involvement of the wider community, this practice of imposing excessive control negates the whole idea of bringing decision making to the people. Decentralization gives room for innovation and creativeness to respond to local conditions. But this is not the case. Practices are more characterized by similarities than diversities as if all ideas originate from one and the same source. This is not to say that anarchy should prevail.

3.4 Community Participation

Community participation is a term that is often used in development vocabulary and is increasingly emphasized. In the field of education, many believe that community engagement in the delivery and management of schooling is crucial. Reflecting the country's new decentralized administrative structure, The Education Sector Strategy released in 1994 explains that the national education system, itself undergoing decentralization, is intended to become more efficient and relevant to the needs of local populations. The strategy emphasizes local engagement, describing how community participation is intended to constitute the final level of the decentralized system. The most obvious form of community participation in both weredas range from the act of enrolling school age children to contributing cash, labour and materials for school infrastructure. To some extent actions related to increasing girls' education opportunities is part of their mandate. The findings show that significant work has been accomplished in school construction (for example, nine new schools in Moretenna Jirru) by raising funds. The fund raised in the latter case totals Birr 212,116.55. The fact that the community shares the burden is quite important. However, community members revealed problems related to over reliance on their contribution and too little support on the part of the government. Parents and school staff commonly contend that the government does not fulfill its responsibilities regarding the school. It is claimed that the community is approached in the majority of the cases for its monetary, material and labour contributions. The effort to involve the community in school administration in the true sense of empowerment is very weak. The present trend of involving the community can not contribute to sustainable development unless the situation is raised to a level where community voices its needs and priorities and participate in decision making. Participation can be meaningful when institutionalized.

3.5 Budgetary Resource and Its Adequacy

Literatures show that many failures in decentralization programs have been attributed to inadequate funding and it has been argued that finance will be the "make or break" factor in decentralization (Asmelash 2000). Both weredas receive a block grant out of which the educational budget is allocated depending on the decision of the concerned wereda council. Within the budget envelope, weredas have full autonomy over how to use the fund from the block grant. The education sector is the highest recipient of budget compared to the other sectors. The major share in the sector, however, goes to wages and salaries. The least percentage represents what is allocated as capital budget. At times there are cases when nothing is allocated as capital budget. The fact that capital budget is minimal or inexistent shows that there is limited means for schools to have important inputs. Schools in both weredas are supposed to receive annually an amount of money calculated on the basis of 10 Birr, 15 Birr and 20 Birr per student for primary first cycle, primary second cycle, and high school, respectively. The above is reported to have been realized in Moretenna Jirru whereas in Bereh Aleltu officials indicated that it is even difficult to allocate 7 Birr per student both for primary first and second cycle because of severe budget constraint. Although it is claimed that budget control has the potential of allowing greater flexibility to meet specific education needs and respond to local problems, this discretion is made available only at the Wereda Education Office level. Schools, which are directly facing problems and are closer to the community, are denied the power of budget control. Because of this, many schools complained that supply of school provisions is delayed and at times they are forced to take supplies, which they have not asked for.

Among the challenges, there are those which are related to school and class room facilities. This situation is contrary to the Education and Training Policy that claims to address the problem of educational quality as one of the main areas of concern (MOE 1994). The Policy qualifies as poor quality the existence of inadequate facilities, insufficient training of teachers and other personnel, overcrowded classes, shortage of books and others. But all the stated problems are widespread in Moretenna Jirru and Bereh Aleltu, which indicates that deep-rooted quality problems prevail. There is an acute budget shortage. Primary education is the number one priority according to the Poverty Reduction Strategy Paper. Whether this can be achieved with the current budget allocation is open to investigation, but given the nature and scale of problems the situation is bleak. Devolution of power is pointless without the corresponding required resource.

Meheret (1998) argues that one of the real tests of an effective self-government is adequate financial strength. Wereda administration in Ethiopia, claims Meheret, are financially strapped mainly because they cannot generate sufficient revenue from local sources. This has meant that their hands are tied when it comes to undertaking meaningful development at the local level. If decentralization should bear fruit, it is indispensable to address the budget resource constraint the study weredas face.

4. Conclusions and Recommendations

Functions such as school construction and establishment, recruitment of school personnel and others, upgrading of schools, budget allocation and execution and some limited pedagogical exercises are devolved to the wereda level both in Moretenna Jirru and Bereh Aleltu. However, major decisions with regard to the above functions are made by a few individuals who are in the executive council, in consultation with officials in the education office. KETBs, PTAs, and school personnel play, in most cases, the role of implementing agents. It may not be an exaggeration to say that the decision making process is characterized more by excessive control than empowerment and this is against the spirit of decentralization.

With regard to human resource, which is critical to the success of decentralization, the Education Office of Moretenna Jirru is found to face a serious problem which has negatively impacted on the service. The situation in Bereh Aleltu is relatively a better one. At the school level human resource problem in terms of qualification number and attitude is observed in both of the study weredas.

KETBs, as a new practice in school administration, are more of a failure than success. KETB members, though expected to provide leadership, lack the educational and relevant experience for the duties and responsibilities they are supposed to carry out. PTAs, which enjoy responsibilities closer to the school level, are rather found to have a better contribution. Overall, the attention given to overcome problems related to human resource development through capacity building program is very insignificant. Given this situation, it is impossible to expect better service just because power is devolved to the district level. One needs to have the relevant qualified personnel.

Communities have demonstrated a willingness to contribute cash, labour and material to support schools. his has made possible the construction of new schools, expansion of existing ones and undertake repair. The above has contributed to increased school enrollment of girls and boys without distinction. The researcher regards this as an achievement, but this is without neglecting the criticism made about the failure in educational quality, which is very critical in development.

The practice of involving the larger community in identifying problems and overall planning activities is almost non-existent. This is incompatible with the objective of decentralization. The support on the part of the community lacks commensurate backing on the part of the government. Without significant assistance from the government, the decentralization effort would be hampered.

The budget in both weredas is mainly absorbed by wages and salaries, reserving minimal or almost nothing for capital investment. It is imperative to provide capacity and financial resources if educational decentralization is to succeed in a sustainable manner without neglecting the already obtained results. In light of the above, it would not be possible for decentralization to take root with the existing capacity gaps. Therefore undertaking major capacity building efforts is indispensable.

In addition, the relationship between the wereda Education Office of both weredas and that of schools is characterized as top-down decision making. School personnel, KETBs and PTAs play the role of implementing agents. It is important that the relationship is redesigned in such a way as to balance flexibility and control and bring empowerment to schools in the long run. Involving the community in matters such as identifying problems, planning and closely monitoring should be ensured. A limitation in community willingness to support schools in an environment where the part done by the government is minimal is increasingly felt. The state should follow a balanced approach as education is basically the responsibility of the state.

Bibliography

Amhara National Regional State. 2003/04-2007/08. Public Sector Capacity
    Building Program Action Plan (PSCAP). Bahir Dar.

Asian Productivity Organization. 2001. Seminar on effective decentralization for
    community development. Summary of proceedings. Colombo, Sri Lanka.

Asmelash Beyene. 2000. Decentralization as a tool for resolving the nationality problem: The Ethiopian experience. *Regional Development Dialogue,* Vol.21, No.1.

Bert Helmsing. 2001. Local economic development in Africa: New generations of actors, policies and instruments. RLDS Working Paper No. 12. Hague: ISS.

Bray, Mark. 1996. *Decentralization of education: Community financing.* Washington, D.C.: World Bank.

Constitution of the Federal Democratic Republic of Ethiopia. 1995. Federal Negarit Gazeta of the Federal Democratic Republic of Ethiopia. Addis Ababa.

Edward, J. Blakley. 1994. *Planning local economic development: Theory and practice.* Newbury Park: Sage.

Federal Democratic Republic of Ethiopia, 2001. Service delivery policy in the civil service. Addis Ababa.

Friske, B. Edward. 1996. *Decentralization of education, politics and consensus.* Washington, D.C.: World Bank.

Gaynor, Cathy. 1998. *Decentralization of education: Teacher management.* Washington, D.C.: International Bank for Reconstruction and Development, World Bank.

Government of the Federal Democratic Republic of Ethiopia. 1999. Education Sector Development Program Action Plan. Addis Ababa.

Gurevich, Robert. 2004. Decentralization in education: Implications at the local level. A paper resented at the Regional and Local Development Studies Seminar, Addis Ababa University. Addis Ababa.

Inter-Africa Group. 2004. Wereda level decentralization in Ethiopia. Experience from some weredas. Addis Ababa.

Litvack, J., .J. Ahmed, and R. Bird. 1998. Rethinking decentralization in developing countries. Washington, D.C.: World Bank.

McGinn. N., and T. Welsh. 1999. *Decentralization of education: Why, when, what and how?* Paris: United Nations Educational, Scientific and Cultural Organization (UNESCO).

Meheret Ayenew. 1998. Some preliminary observations on institutional and administrative gaps in Ethiopia's decentralization process. Working Paper No.1. Addis Ababa: Regional and Local Development Studies, Addis Ababa University.

Ministry of Education. 2002. Educational management/ organization, community participation and financing guideline. Addis Ababa. Unpublished.

Ministry of Finance and Economic Development (MOFED). 2002/03. Ethiopia: Sustainable development and poverty reduction (SDPRP). Addis Ababa.

Rondinelli A., R. John Nellis, and Shabbir G. Cheema. 1983. *Decentralization in developing countries: A review of recent experience.* Washington, D.C.: World Bank.

Piriou, Suzanne Sall. 1998. *Decentralization and rural development: A review of evidence.* Washington, D.C.: World Bank.

Tassew Woldehanna and Eberlei Walter. 2004. Pro-poor budgeting and the role of parliament in the implementation of PRSP in Ethiopia. German Technical Cooperation and Department of Economics, Addis Ababa University. Addis Ababa.

Swift-Morgan, Jennifer. 2004 Community participation: So what? Paper presented at the conference of Comparative and International Education Society, Salt Lake City, UT.

Tegegne Gebre-Egziabher and Kassahun Berhanu. 2004. The role of decentralized governance in building local institutions, diffusing ethnic conflicts, and alleviating poverty in Ethiopia. *Regional Development Dialogue,* Vol. 25, no.1.

United Nations (UN). 2000. *Redesigning methods and procedures for the delivery of local services in small island countries.* Department of Economic and Social Affairs. New York: UN.

Winkler, R. Donald. 1989. *Decentralization in education: An economic perspective.* Population and Human Resources Department. Washington, D.C.: World Bank.

World Bank. 1997, Rational for decentralization. http://www.ciein.org/decentralization/entryway/sitelinddex.htm/.

V

The Performance of Wereda Decentralization Program in Amhara National Regional State: With Emphasis on Legambo Wereda in South Wello Zone[*]

Muhammed Seid Yimer

1. Introduction

Good governance has been taken as a solution for different types of problems now-a-days in many countries of the world. One of the peculiar features of good governance is democratic decentralization or devolution of power to local level of governments. The 1990s are considered as a period of democratic decentralization with a number of implementation impediments especially in Africa (Loop 2002, 7-8). Although the debate still continues, it has become a worldwide belief that decentralization will help to overcome different socio- economic and political problems.

The foundation of real decentralization in Ethiopia could be traced back to the transition period. It was declared that the right of every nation, nationality and people of Ethiopia to self-determination has been affirmed (*Negarit Gazeta* No.1 July 1991). This was reaffirmed with more elaboration by the FDRE Constitution as the basis of the federal system of government. Such fundamental rights included, among others, the right to preserve identity, to promote own culture and history and to administer own affairs within a defined own territory. It is very clear that decentralization couldn't be practical in real terms unless devolution of power to local level governments is exercised. Although the decentralized system of governance is aimed at bringing about political stability and sustainable development in Ethiopia, it is still at a very early stage and thus demands a great deal of effort for realizing significant changes. As decentralization is a very complex process, it is too difficult to implement it unless there is minimum capacity to begin with.

---

[*] This chapter is based on the author's MA Thesis submitted to the Institute of Regional and Local Development Studies, Addis Ababa University, 2006.

According to the International Monetary Fund (February 2004), untied block grants from regional governments to the districts have been introduced following local level decentralization. The decentralization program includes improvements in the planning, budgeting, financial disbursement, accounting, reporting and monitoring systems. Although the district level fiscal decentralization process is well managed due to flexible as well as practical assistance from regional level offices in the four regions, constraints are impeding the process. The government also recognizes that the short-term and long-term challenges of power decentralization to district level are part of the "learning-by-doing process" and continuous commitment is an essential factor for success from all citizens and from partners.

According to the International Monetary Fund and my own personal observation, the first and most challenging problem of the wereda level decentralization program is lack of skilled humanpower. The second problem relates to budget limitation; inability to pay monthly salaries has been experienced in some weredas following local level fiscal decentralization. The third and fourth main problem, which impedes the decentralization process, is associated with unelaborated legal provisions and issues of improper structure. Therefore, a study should be undertaken to assess the current performance of the program along with identifying the magnitude of the above mentioned problems and other drawbacks in order to take timely corrective measures. It is the research hypothesis that most of the local level civil servants and even the political leadership lack the capacity to understand and implement the decentralization program in a proper manner and as planned. In the absence of well-designed capacity building measures and training scheme, as well as appropriate institutional setups, for direct implementers and indirect supporters of the policy, the wereda decentralization program may hinder prospects for realizing stated goals rather than facilitating their actualization. Investigating the problem calls for an area-specific study so as to have a deeper understanding of the practicality and performance of the decentralization drives. This study was conducted in the Amhara National Regional State, with the emphasis on Legambo Wereda in South Wello Zone.

The general objectives of this research is to assess the program's performance, to identify impediments that affect the process, and then to propos solutions for the problems by way of recommendation. The specific objectives include: reviewing the major components and implementation of the wereda level decentralization and empowerment program, reviewing and analyzing the gaps in peoples' participation in relation to local empowerment and decentralization, assessing the competence and commitment of officials and other civil servants regarding the current decentralization drive in the research location, and identifying major impediments affecting the decentralization process so that appropriate solutions could be proposed.

The study uses a qualitative approach, which is based on an assumption or a hypothesis. Qualitative research occurs in natural settings where human behaviours and events occur and an attempt is made to understand multiple realities. This approach also focuses on processes and outcomes (Mwanje 2001). As wereda decentralization is an on-going program, its components interact with other development programs of the country. Given that the research focuses on the performance of the on-going decentralization and the competence of program implementers, the qualitative approach is relevant for this study.

The study was held in 2005 and 2006. Data were collected from primary and secondary sources. Primary data were collected through unstructured interviews with focus groups and key informants. The key informants are government officials and technical experts at regional, zonal, and wereda levels. Besides, NGOs that have stakes and are actively participating in development effort in the study locality are also involved as informants. The participants of the focus group discussions were relevant civil servants in the wereda pertinent offices and influential community members who include: indigenous community organization leaders, religious leaders, and civic association leaders in the study wereda. Statistical documents, minutes, formal reports and unpublished documents from different offices including Regional, Zonal and Wereda government offices were used as source secondary data. The data were updated through telephone conversation and other communication technologies. Secondary data were also collected from books, journals, working papers, previous studies, etc.

2. Theoretical Considerations

The term decentralization has different meanings for different people. However, it is mostly used to express relations of authority and responsibility and also includes several complex issues. Most authors on the subject agree that decentralization means transfer of authority and responsibility from higher to lower government bodies and functionaries. There are different approaches of transferring authority and responsibility. Among these, administrative, political, fiscal and economic decentralization are the main ones (Boro 2002; Nahu 2004; House of Federation 2002).

Generally speaking, decentralization has many roles to play in solving political, administrative and economic problems. It is used to reduce overload and congestion in administration and communication. As a result of effective decentralization, quantity and quality of service provision could be improved. Providing some sort of decision-making power to local managers could facilitate improvement in service provision. Public participation could also be promoted by increasing the involvement of stakeholders either on their own or through their representatives. Besides, decentralization is a way of achieving self-reliance and self-determination as political objectives of citizens. Decentralization, in one way or other, can assume different forms: deconcentration, delegation, devolution, as well as privatization or deregulation (Rondineli *et al.* in Eshetu 1994, 1; House of Federation 2002).

Boro (2002) regards deconcentration, delegation or devolution as types or forms of administrative decentralization. According to him, political decentralization focuses on devolution of decision-making power by creating sub-national governments through election in a multi-party system. It also includes enjoying fiscal autonomy in a territorial jurisdiction. Mehret (1998) on his part focuses on political and administrative forms as the major approaches of decentralization. According to him, political decentralization is a way of responding to political pressure for self-ruling authority. It also includes defined area of jurisdiction for self-administration. The guarantee for practice on self-rule is the conducting of democratic elections periodically.

The idea of political decentralization is not limited only to self-rule but also includes accountability, responsiveness, equity, justice and representation in political life. Besides, institutional settings and fiscal authority are also important. Political decentralization also includes the legitimacy of local governments through election as well as fiscal autonomy for self- development and self- determination (Mehret 1998; Boro 2002).

Mehret also states that administrative decentralization is a hierarchical division of labor between headquarters and field offices. Administrative decentralization refers to delegation of function and authority, and can be revoked by the center whenever it is necessary. The primary objective of such kind of decentralization is promoting efficiency by allocating resources centrally with guidelines that govern priorities. So, applying policies and rules uniformly is the working principle of administrative decentralization. Boro (2002) says that the aim of administrative decentralization is to transfer responsibility for planning, financing and managing public functions with semi-autonomous authority in the form of deconcentration or delegation.

The decentralization drive in Ethiopia that is currently underway is more of political due to the fact that it focuses on self-rule and empowerment (Mehret 1998). Such devolution of power as is currently taking place in Ethiopia includes not only self-rule but also fiscal autonomy and has a constitutional base as its guarantee against undue interference. So, the preference of political decentralization over administrative decentralization marks the current Ethiopian decentralization process.

Therefore, the conceptual framework for this research paper about implementation and performance is political decentralization (devolution) at the wereda-level in Amhara National Regional State.

3. ANRS Wereda Decentralization Program Performance

Although the wereda decentralization program's long-term driving force is the Federal Constitution, the urgent launch of the program since 1995 E.C. is the result of EPRDF's Renewal Movement. Regional and zonal government officials reiterate that although a federal structure was launched previously, there was no deep-rooted understanding about aspects of decentralization and implementation mechanisms at lower level administrative hierarchies. However, although the decentralization program started with minimum capacity and level of understanding, constraints have been solved through time under the principle of "learning by doing".

Discussions with focus groups, especially indigenous community organizations ("idirs") and religious institutions confirm that they have no idea about the decentralization program till now. Most of them could not tell the difference between pre- and post-decentralization governance systems. Such outcomes imply that there is limitation in enlightening the people about the decentralization program itself to create a situation of grassroots initiative for change. Some respondents, especially technical experts, argue extreme urgency results in lack of knowledge and understanding about performing procedures and instruments. Thus, one can conclude that although there is not much doubt about improvement in their commitment to exercise their authority and responsibility independently, local government's political leaderships have had serious limitations in terms of competence until now.

3.1 Performance of Medium-term Wereda Decentralization Components

District Level Decentralization Program (wereda decentralization) is one of the major capacity building programs in the public sector. As decentralization is a complex process determined by interactive factors, the current policy of decentralization has different aspects that should have been implemented in an integrated manner. These include: deepening devolution of power to lower tiers of regional governance, strengthening institutional decision-making power to enhance democratic participation, promoting good governance, improving service delivery, and contributing to poverty reduction and sustainable development as well as creating a viable development center at wereda level (Worku 2004). These interventions can be categorized in to three main medium-term activity components to make the analysis easier and comprehensive. These are institutional and organizational setups, fiscal decentralization and service delivery.

3.2 Performance of Institutional and Organizational Setups

Institutional and organizational setup aspect sub-divisions include power devolution and restructuring, personnel deployment and training, pool system application and access to facilities. The performance of each of the sub-divisions is as follows.

3.2.1 Performance of Power Devolution and Restructuring

Contrary to the provision of the sub-Article 50(4) of the Federal Constitution, devolution of power to local governments has been curtailed for the last ten years. However, the ANRS' Amended Constitution (1994 E.C) not only separated the three branches of government at each level, but also clearly defined their responsibility as well as authority. The decentralization program limits the power of zone administrations for the sake of promoting local-level self-rule.

However, such a shift of power has its own limitations in practice. As the authority and responsibility of non-ethnic based zone structures is limited to give support to wereda structures only on requests, their personnel were reduced as much as possible to minimize costs. It was assumed that focal personnel in zonal structures can facilitate the working relations between weredas and the Region without affecting local governments' self- administration power, which has direct accountability to the Regional Government. Besides, although there is a cabinet type structure at the zonal level, it doesn't include the main public service sectors such as education and health. Due to the narrowness of the personnel structure, weak financial capacity and diminished power, zone structures have become passive conduits for information flow rather than playing supportive and facilitation roles as intended. Worku (2004) states in this respect that zonal structures are not "points of decision-making" following the wereda-level decentralization.

Due to the above-mentioned facts, regional offices have been facing work pressure and congestion. Wereda offices couldn't get responses or feedbacks for their requests on time from regional offices. Therefore, it has become clear that to be used as a bridge between the weredas and the Regional Government, zonal offices should be strengthened and capacitated to some extent. This is because not only is the Region very wide with a large population, but also there is limited technical capacity and technological base at each level, which justifies the important roles to be played by zonal structures.

Therefore, an initiative has been taken by the Head of the Regional Government to bring about consensus among all concerned parties about the indispensable role of zonal structures. A business process reengineering has begun in some offices to make zonal structures capable of playing their roles. Such business process reengineering includes assessing the appropriateness of office personnel structure compared to their mandate, and the absence of duplication of mandates, and gaps among offices. This results not only in strengthening the zonal administrations' power in relative terms, but also in expanding the cabinet structure by including important sectors. Still, there is another critical problem facing zonal structures for them to perform their tasks properly. This relates to the supply of trained personnel in the market and the problem of maximum turnover that is aggravated from time to time.

Prior to wereda decentralization, the power to review the Regional Constitution was given to the Regional Council. Now, such power is given to an independent organ called Constitutional Interpreting Commission (CIC), which comprises representatives of wereda council members. The Commission holds meetings when necessary in accordance with the provisions of the amended Regional Constitution. Such power shift is aimed at creating a system of check and balance between the Regional Council and wereda councils to safeguard local governments' self-administration authority as much as possible.

On the other hand, appointment of judges to first instance courts is still the power of the Regional Council. Wereda respondents argue that such provision contradicts with their self-administration power, i.e., it limits the authority of wereda councils to appoint judges in their jurisdiction. However, it is underlined in the Regional Constitution that although local units have full self-administration and development authority in running their internal affairs, wereda administrations are not only accountable to the Regional Government but also considered as a subordinate body of the Regional Government. In a decentralized system of governance, there is always some power reserved to the central organ to promote common interests and values. Still, it should be recognized that citizens have more stake in the judiciary at any level and any where in the Region than in other institutions.

The Region is criticized for wereda judicial system's non-responsiveness to pubic comments regarding efficiency of service delivery. Wereda respondents argue that such non-responsiveness of wereda judicial bodies to people's criticisms is a result of their lack of accountability to the wereda people and/or their representatives. They argue that there should be a mechanism for balancing the interest of the people and the independence of the judiciary in terms of accountability for service delivery. At present, a partial solution is being sought through requiring presidents of wereda first instance courts to submit activity reports to their pertinent wereda councils. However, councils have no power to take action, with the exception of making recommendations.

The Legambo Wereda administration is structured into 34 peasant associations and two urban kebeles. The three branches of government (executive, council and judiciary) are organized independently at wereda and kebele levels. The Wereda has 105 Council members. Council members are directly elected from each kebele by a quota system on the basis of population size. Women's participation in the Council is only 27%. The Council has its own speaker, deputy speaker and five standing committees. The responsibility for overseeing day-to-day activities is that of the speaker. Committees are established on a sector basis. The Committees' mandate is to submit a follow-up report on the performance of executive offices and other related issues to the Council's meetings. Each standing committee of the council has three members and all except two members of the committee are fulltime civil servants in the executive offices. The question here is, how can the members of a standing committee perform their duties effectively and independently as the people's representatives when they are fulltime employees of the executive offices? Besides, although there is a common understanding that legislative organs should be independent from any sort of influence by the executive bodies to ensure efficiency and accountability, the Legislative Council is still dependent on the Executive Council for support staff and other facilities which makes it practically an extension of the later.

According to the Government Structure Taskforce (1994 E.C.), the core mission of wereda executive structures that are put in place following the decentralization scheme is transforming the agricultural sector. It also takes into consideration that different wereda sector offices should be relatively independent to perform their mission effectively and efficiently. The wereda administration executive body is restructured into ten independent offices. Some of the offices are newly established ones that include Capacity Building, Information, and Public Participation and Organization Affairs offices. Others are Agriculture and Rural Development, Finance and Planning, Administrative and Security Affairs, Trade and Industry (Small & Micro Enterprises), Health, Justice, and Youth, Culture and Sport Affairs. Each of these has its own sub-structures as required. And there were seven members of the Wereda Executive Council (Cabinet), including the Chief Administrator and the deputy. Each member, excluding the Chief Administrator, is the head of the main executive line office, such as Capacity Building, Information, Public Participation and Organization Affairs, Agriculture and Rural Development,

Youth, Culture and Sport Affairs, Administration and Security Affairs Offices. There is only one female in the cabinet of the study wereda.

There are institutional gaps here and there with respect to accountability, and appropriateness in the wereda administration Executive Structure. For instance, health and education offices are represented by capacity building offices in the wereda cabinets; however, finance and planning, and trade and industry have no proper representation in the cabinets. Besides, the personnel structure in some offices was not properly studied during the restructuring, and there is mismatch here and there.

The other serious challenge in the wereda executive offices, in addition to the gaps mentioned above, is lack of qualified personnel. For instance, the Finance and Planning Office in the study wereda has no experienced and skilled staff for planning activities. Thus, although an integrated development planning is the mandate of this office, the office left this responsibility to each sector office of the wereda. Secondly, there is no common and clear understanding about the role of the mandates of newly established offices among the wereda sector offices themselves and the public at large. It is surprising that these newly established offices are considered more politically affiliated to the government, and hence highly trained professionals are not willing to join them, although there is some improvement through time in this respect.

Following the 2005 National Election, the government has noted the drawbacks of wereda structures, and subsequently restructuring measures have been taken. The number of cabinet members in the wereda executive structure has almost been doubled by including important sectors such as education, health, finance and planning, trade and industry, and women's affairs. On the other hand, Public Participation and Organization Affairs office was demoted to an advisory expert role although the expert remains a member of the cabinet.

3.2.2 Performance of Personnel Deployment and Training

One of the mechanisms to capacitate rural weredas with skilled and experienced humanpower is by deploying personnel from regional and zonal offices. However, due to lack of clarity of the directives and some times due to negligence, the desired objective of capacitating rural weredas by deploying personnel has not been achieved. Even though the primary objective of the deployment program was to strengthen rural weredas, most of the deployed personnel were not highly trained and experienced technical experts but support staff, especially guards and janitors. Besides, a number of deployed personnel were rushed to weredas which are located near big towns. Thus, remote weredas could not benefit from the deployment exercise contrary to the intended objective. The failure of the staff deployment scheme as mentioned above creates personnel disparity among weredas instead of narrowing existing gaps. An imbalance was also created between support and technical expert staff in weredas receiving newly deployed personnel. In extreme cases, some weredas such as Kutaber in South Wello Zone, were not able to pay even the salary of civil servants due to such unexpected rush in transfers, for which budgetary allocations were not made.

As wereda decentralization program is a learning-by-doing scheme, there was expectation that an intensive training aimed at intra-wereda capacity building would be implemented seriously. However, weredas couldn't perform the training by themselves till now due to lack of appropriate institutional setups such as rules and regulations, as well as lack of professional (technical) assistance from above. However, it is expected that these constraints would be tackled in the course of time.

Wereda officials reported that they had access to some training and other working manuals to facilitate the decentralization mission. However, they complained that the manuals are not prepared in a systematic manner in addition to the absence of intensive training on the manuals themselves for ease of implementation. Besides, there are frequent changes of directives and guidelines that affect consistency and continuity in application. Moreover, although there are a number of training programs at the regional level on issues pertinent to decentralization targeting wereda staff members, trainings were given in a piece meal and haphazard manner. The nature of the trainings that have been organized by wereda government structures themselves in relation to major strategies and policies of the country, such as rural development, are more of introducing the government's interest and policy direction rather than taking into account public views and preferences on how to improve the policies and plans of the government.

3.2.3 Performance and Application of the Pool System

Following wereda level decentralization, government office restructuring in ANRS followed an innovative approach by applying a pool system. Finance service is under a single pool system. Besides, wereda executive offices are categorized into four groups to share clerical personnel and material support services. The pool system has different advantages according to most respondents. Some of the advantages of the pool system are: minimizing workload of technical experts, minimizing administrative and procurement costs, minimizing corruption by maximizing transparency, and maximizing the productivity of personnel who work in pool service units.

However, the pool service system has its drawbacks. First and foremost, different offices have different capacity to submit their demand (for instance, procurement need) on time, and this creates unnecessary delays of work. Secondly, qualified personnel in most cases do not occupy key personnel positions of the pool service. Such gaps hampered the efficiency and work quality of not only the pool service but also the performance of the whole service delivery system. Wereda government officials are trying to use short-term solutions to the problem of shortage of qualified personnel, that is, the vacant post is filled with temporarily transferred personnel or additional responsibility is given to an employee beyond his/her regular duty. It is argued that, heavy workload, not accompanied by incentives and inappropriate placement of staff lead to frustration, anxiety, and departure of staff in extreme causes.

3.2.4. Performance in Access to Facilities

Supply of office furniture and vehicles from zonal offices was one of the measures to achieve the objective of creating conducive working environment in wereda offices. However, such deployment has only a limited contribution for the intended goal due to the fact that most of the furniture and the vehicles were not only very old but also have serious damages that require more money to repair and put to use. Wereda political leaderships used different alternatives to tackle office and other facility constraints by themselves. Constructing new offices and buying the necessary furniture through own budget and/or with external assistance could bring about significant achievements. However, the extreme case in this respect is related to buying expensive furniture in the face of considerable budgetary constraints.

Although there is improvement in vehicles access, as a result of the wereda decentralization program, there is still a shortage and lack of vehicles in the study wereda, which is a more serious problem in some offices. Besides, the access of modern office equipment such as fax machines and computers is a burning issue in almost all the rural weredas of South Wello Zone. Although there is telephone access in all weredas, the system is backward in some cases. Besides, the wereda-net program is not yet fully operational.

3.2.5 Performance in Fiscal Decentralization

Fiscal decentralization is one of the main dimensions of power sharing. This is because fiscal decentralization governs the whole spectrum of different level of inter-governmental relations. Besides, fiscal decentralization focuses not only on the principle of cost-benefit analysis, but also on sensitive public issues to achieve the objective of creating stable and democratic governance. As the wereda is the most important local government unit in the Ethiopian case for entrenching good governance, devolution of power to wereda governments would be meaningless without fiscal decentralization. Thus, the ANRS wereda decentralization program (the so-called second wave of decentralization) has a significant role in bringing about change through fiscal dimensions.

However, there is still a great gap in addressing problems associated with financing of grassroots level government structures. Although kebele administrations are the lowest government tiers for direct service delivery and administration, they are the most neglected prior to and after the commencement of the decentralization drive. The only source of money for a typical rural kebele administration is social court files. However, there are pilot projects of fiscal decentralization at the kebele level that was sponsored and technically assisted by external donors. Still, there is a counterpart argument that in the current context of the Region (due to institutional, financial and human resource limitations), it is impossible to exercise fiscal decentralization at the kebele level.

The fiscal dimension of the wereda decentralization program (block grant transfers), created an enabling environment for local governments to administer transferred budget without the interference of higher tiers. Besides, funding agencies should negotiate and reach a consensus with wereda administrations about their project before dealing with the Regional Disaster Prevention and Preparedness Commission Office. Such a privilege is creating a fertile ground to address people's primary needs although it is not yet fully practical. Wereda administrations also have the authority to hire, administer and fire their civil servants in accordance with the civil service law of the Region.

Before wereda decentralization, regional transfers were directly allocated to zonal administrations after which the zones allocate the money to weredas under them. The allocation system is mostly subjective and lacks transparency as well as fairness. Following the wereda decentralization schemes, the Regional State's total amount of money originated from federal transfers, Regional State's own revenue, sub-regional state's own revenue; external funding (assistance or loan) is allocated directly to the weredas by using the block grant formula. Following the decentralization, zonal structures became part of the regional structures in all aspects and have no decisive role to play in fiscal transfers.

The application of wereda block grant formula in ANRS was a new concept for most government officials. As a result, the first trial was simply adopting the federal system with some adjustment. According to BoFED (April 2004), the ANRS' previous block grant formula included: population size, development disparity and own revenue performance indexes only.

Consequently, unexpected problems were faced in the process of implementing wereda level decentralization. When a budget was allocated to weredas using a block grant formula for the first time in ANRS in 1995 E.C. fiscal year, some weredas especially those located near big towns and those which have small population size, faced great difficulty.

Disparities in development level and population size indicators favor those weredas which have limited infrastructure and large population size while minimizing the amount of budget transferred to those weredas with better infrastructure and small population size. On the contrary, weredas that have better infrastructure naturally seek more funds to run effectively the infrastructures they have. This was the major limitation of the block grant formula from the beginning. The new block grant formula, which was launched as of 1997 E.C. fiscal year, includes population size, own revenue competence and development disparity indexes but also recurrent expenditure need. The new block grant formula gives a weight of 50 percent for population, 15 percent for recurrent expenditure need, 20 percent for own revenue collection performance, and 15 percent for development disparity indexes.

However, the new block grant formula is premature due to the fact that there is no credible data that could serve as the bases for calculating each wereda's exact position for the indexes. Besides, there is still a significant gap to cover the expenditure need of each wereda although it is a countrywide problem. In addition, the participation of local governments in the process of budget transfer is limited to only providing relevant information. Although fiscal transfer criteria are made official through print media of the regional government, it doesn't ensure transparency by itself. Zonal and wereda respondents urge that besides ensuring transparency, there should also be direct and meaningful involvement on the part of local governments in the fiscal transfer processes. At least a kind of budget hearing forum before approval, that accommodates local governments' views and preferences, could be one alternative solution for addressing the problem.

Concerning the experience of the study Wereda (Legambo), there was no serious challenge in relation to budget demand and supply gap following the fiscal decentralization. This is due to the fact that on one hand, Legambo Wereda is a relatively remote area; personnel deployed from regional and zonal offices were not assigned to the Wereda save some floated staff from merged weredas. On the other hand, the Legambo Wereda has an average number of population compared to other weredas with limited infrastructural position. Both of these indexes favor the Wereda in block grant transfer. The block grants transferred to the Legambo Wereda are about 5.54 million and 5.52 million Birr in 1993 and 1994 E.C, respectively. Then, it rises to 6.41 million, 7.06 million, 10.03 million and

12.19 million Birr in consecutive years following the fiscal decentralization measure.

Besides, the improved external assistance as well as federal special fund flow to the study wereda was due its chronic problem of food insecurity and very poor infrastructure. That covers the government budget demand and supply gap.   For instance, a significant amount (Birr 5,472,252.00 and Birr 5,856,499.00) of external and federal special fund was obtained by the Legambo Wereda in 1996 and 1997 E.C., respectively. However, there are challenges in integrating such funds with the government budget and with the priorities of the people.   From a total external and federal special fund flow to the Legambo Wereda in 1997 E. C, 71% went to the agriculture sector, 7% to the health sector, 6% to the education sector, and 12% to others. The rationale for the inclination of funding agencies towards the agricultural sector is to strengthen the effort towards food security and food self-sufficiency. However, Wereda officials argue that if there is fund distribution among different sectors, it will help to address people's needs and utilization of budget efficiently and effectively.

The revenue assignment of wereda structures include: personal income tax, rural land use fee and agricultural income tax, as well as fee from license and service charges. The share of own revenue from the block grant transferred in the Legambo Wereda was 24 percent in 1993, 1994 and 1995 E.C. However, the share of the Wereda income from block grant transferred increased to 27 percent in 1996, 1997, and 1998 E.C. Nevertheless, such data implies that the Legambo Wereda is mostly dependent not only on subsidy but also on the external as well as federal special fund for its development activities. This is due to the fact that a significant number of the people (38 percent) are below the poverty line. However, the capacity limitations of the wereda structure to exploit any available opportunity to maximize own revenue is still a major limitation.

Decentralized system of governance is aimed at shifting not only authority but also responsibility for self-development to the people. Decentralized system of governance encourages sustainable resource generation due to active and voluntary participation of the people. The resource generated from society can be in the form of labor, cash or in kind as well as professional assistance. There was no practice of projecting expected resources that can be generated from the society until wereda decentralization   program   implementation.   Following   Wereda decentralization people are contributing their share in poverty reduction-related programs such as education and health services, environmental conservation and the like, which is very encouraging for sustainable development. All type of public contribution calculated in terms of money was about half compared with the government budget in 1995 E C. and it was two-fold in 1996 E.C. It rises to around four-fold in 1997 and 1998 E.C.

If such a trend continues, there is no doubt that the Region may register significant development in the near future. The question here is, is such public participation sustainable and, is it made on a voluntary basis? This is because some of the focus group discussants explained that without creating a genuine environment for involvement in local development planning from the beginning, they were simply told to do this and to do that by local officials. The people are not well informed about the guarantee of an active and sustainable participation. Worku (1994 E. C.), conclude that the people are not active participants in wereda development planning, and that there is no significant change regarding participation of the public in local development planning both before and after the wereda decentralization. NGO respondents on their part explained that mobilizing the people for local development is not scientific and systematic. Officials use only formal governmental structures rather than make use of indigenous community institutions.

Although government officials could not concur with the view of the stakeholders until recently, they are obliged to recognize the fact following the 2005 National Election. The government opens public forums just following the election and it is learnt from the forums that there was reluctance on the side of the government in considering public interests and in enduring voluntary participation. Although there are village and kebele level consultation meetings about performance in development planning, they were mostly for formality rather than for genuine involvement of the people. Although important comments come out as feedback from the community here and there, the comments are not reaching higher political leaderships through the proper channels until recently.

One of the main outcomes expected from fiscal decentralization is ensuring efficiency and equity in intra-wereda budget planning at local level. Following wereda decentralization, each wereda receives its untied block grant budget directly from the Region. Generally speaking, there is great focus on pro-poor activities in wereda government budget planning in such area as education, agriculture and health. Such pro-poor planning trend developed through time by considering the major development strategies of the country and the targets set by the Millennium Development Goals. Besides, there is great care for pre-commitment expenditure such as salary and already launched projects. However, there are no clearly articulated and compiled budget planning and administration procedures, directives and standards in line with the implementation of decentralization program for all sectors.

Each of the Wereda offices, including the Legislative Council, tries to exercise their budget plan and predict their financial needs after which they send the same to the Wereda Finance and Planning Office. The Wereda Finance and Planning Office collects budget plan documents from each sector office and adjusts it in accordance with the ceiling set by the Regional Finance Bureau, and then submits it to the Cabinet for discussion. After the approval of the budget plan by the Wereda Legislative Council, the Wereda Finance and Planning Office makes a written budget announcement to each sector office on items of approved expenditures and total allocation made to each. Here, it should be noted that the budget of the wereda first instance courts is transferred directly from the Regional Supreme Court. Contingency budget is strictly forbidden in wereda budget planning throughout the Region. The rationale is to prevent financial mismanagement. However, there is a possibility of revising the budget plan in the mean time. The Executive Council can revise the recurrent budget of each office. Capital budget revision authority is the mandate of the Legislative Council.

In such financial planning processes, there is no procedure that assures public consultation, a phenomenon that is contrary to the principle of local democracy. Besides, there is a problem of quality goods supply in procurement mostly due to limitation of experience and knowledge as well as due to negligence among the procurement staff. Moreover, the problem of ensuring credible financial and store management system administration has surfaced in the decentralization program. Due to weak internal and external audit as well as store management system, there is an indication that resources are abused in some weredas. For instance, the Agriculture and Rural Development Office in the study wereda is under investigation in this respect.

There was a practice of undertaking external audit on every office of a wereda prior to the introduction of financial single pool system. That is, wereda finance and planning offices were responsible for the application of external audit on other intra-wereda line offices. However, as financial service is now under a single pool system in wereda government structures performed by the finance and planning offices of each wereda, it is not possible to perform a genuine external audit. Besides, although there is a General Auditor at the regional level, its role is limited in this respect due to capacity and other related problems. Thus, there is a gap in ensuring credible intra-wereda financial audit system now-a-days in ARS wereda administration. Therefore, either an independent intra-wereda auditing organ should be established or the General Auditor of the Region should perform an external audit on each wereda administration to fill the gap in this respect.

3.2.6 Services Delivery Performance

Following wereda decentralization, the responsibility of wereda structures for service delivery is clearly articulated. This includes primary education service, basic health care service, agricultural extension service, veterinary service, land-use rights administration, water development, well construction and maintenance, local police service, and local roads access. A remarkable measure that has been taken in parallel with wereda decentralization in ANRS is the civil service reform that aimed at improving public service delivery. Although it is not the main agenda of this research to deal with, the Civil Service Reform has serious impacts on the service delivery performance and decentralization program achievements. Side-by-side with the wereda decentralization program, each wereda office has been launching the Civil Service Reform program in one way or another. Among the components of the civil service reform program that have a significant impact for the decentralization schemes, launching a strategic plan for each office and service sub-program, quality improvement can be mentioned. However, the strategic plan of each office could not meet the expected quality standards, as it is a recent phenomenon.

To achieve the desired goal of improving service delivery, special units are established in each office. Such units are responsible for addressing issues of complaints. Besides, there is an evaluation forum called *"gimgema"* that is held periodically and at any time as necessary. The objective of the forum ("gimgema") is to encourage those who register good performance and to criticize those who have had bad records in their performance. Such approach is very helpful in terms of experience sharing and in terms of ensuring accountability. However, some people have a negative attitude towards such forums ("gimgema"). They argue that its implementation is full of subjectivity due to lack of standardized performance indicators and procedures. Besides, there is no material incentive for good achievers. The counter argument is that some personnel have attitudinal problem to appreciate and encourage change in this respect. Thus, further investigation should be done on the issue to establish underlying causes.

The other challenge relating to service quality is the incidence of frequent turnover among the political leadership and the civil servants. For instance, one of the study wereda cabinet members' positions changed three times within two years. Besides, three head posts shifted hands to run the Capacity Building Office of the study wereda within two years. Respondents from NGOs underline that the problem of frequent turnover among government higher officials and civil servants has been creating a gap in terms of reaching common understanding about their projects.

3.2.6.1 Performance in Education

As primary education is one of the main missions of local governments, it is found that Legambo Wereda registered good performance in terms of expansion although there is a reservation with respect to quality. Primary education enrollment ration was about 61% in 1994 and 1995 E.C. However, a radical change has been registered in primary education enrollment performance since 1996 E.C., that is, 75.68, 90.97 and 97 percent, respectively in 1996, 1997 and 1998 E.C. Such figures do not include the alternative basic education services aimed at reaching children and youth out of the regular system. The drastic improvement in primary education enrollment since 1996 E.C. is due to the immense efforts exerted to achieve the Millennium Development Goals; i.e., the wereda officials, especially the political leaderships, were able to motivate and mobilize the people at the grassroots level using public conferences and other forums.

However, such achievement could not be replicated in the areas of quality although there is some improvement. That is, teacher-student ratio was 1:82 in 1994 E.C; it is 1:71 in 1998 E.C. The classroom-student ratio was 1:85 in 1994; it is 1:73 in 1998 E C. Concerning textbook-student ratio, it is still a serious problem although there is some improvement after the decentralization program. It was 1: 4 until 1995 E.C. It has improved to 1:3, and 1:2 in 1997 and 1998 E.C., respectively.

On the other hand, the outcome of the effort to decrease the ratio of dropouts is encouraging. It was 4.1 and 7.6 percent in 1994 and 1995 E.C. academic years, respectively. However, it comes down to 1.7, 1.23, and 0.4 percent in 1996, 1997 and 1998 E.C., respectively. In terms of repeaters' ratio at the primary level, there was a serious problem previously. That is repeaters' ratio was 19.95 and 23.7 percent in 1994 and 1995 E.C., respectively. However, it dramatically decreased to 2.43, 1.83 and, 2.16 percent in 1996, 1997 and 1998 E.C. It can be stated, though with serious reservations, that this achievement seems very encouraging. How such an achievement can be regarded as commendable in the face of serious quality-related problems or whether there is any change in the promotion policy, are some of the questions that must be posed and answered. On the other hand, although primary education enrollment ratio is encouraging for both sexes in Legambo Wereda, the decentralization program could not bring about a significant improvement in narrowing the gender gap. That is, the gender gap on average has been around 7 percent for the last three years.

3.2.6.2 Performance of the Health Sector

Local governments are the most immediate structures for the implementation of the health sector strategy, which is prevention rather than treatment. Although previous years' relevant data are not available in the study wereda to compare, both potable water supply and health service coverage ratio reached 32, 44.3 and 51.67 % in 1996, 1997 and 1998 E.C., respectively. The health service area coverage was 32 percent in 1996 E. C. However, it rose to 43.23 and 69.8 percent in 1997 and 1998 E.C. due to the newly constructed health institutions. Still, there is a serious problem in relation to service quality due to acute shortage of trained personnel. Besides, health institutions are below standard in terms of their facility. Although there is a significant improvement in terms of health service area coverage following decentralization due to local government initiation in constructing primary health institutions, it could not guarantee the improvement of service coverage in this respect.

3.2.6.3 Performance of the Agricultural Sector

Until recently, agricultural extension service in the Region was targeted towards increasing production by focusing on agronomy (supply of modern inputs such as fertilizer and improved seeds). However, the performance of agricultural extension service delivery was very poor viewed in the light of the emphasis given to the sector in the study wereda. The participants in the minimum extension service package in Legambo Wereda were 5290 households, out of close to forty four thousands households in the wereda, in 1993 E.C. This figure comes down to 1,312, 1,902 and 739 in 1994, 1995 and 1996 E.C., respectively. Then, the number of participants in minimum package rises to 16,445 and 16,532 in 1997 and 1998 E.C., respectively, in parallel with the family package. That is, the minimum package should go in parallel with a new package called "Family Package" since 1996 E.C. The participants in the new package families in Legambo Wereda were 6,944, 3,702 and 5,002, respectively, in 1996, 1997 and 1998 E.C.

Concerning the production trend, annual production was 154,680.0 quintals (0.93 quintal/head) and 187,955.3 quintals (1.11 quintal/head) in 1994 and 1995 E.C., respectively. It increased to 226,886.0 quintals (1.33 quintal/head), 354,791 quintals (2.0 quintal/head) and 508,380 quintals (2.8 quintal/head) in 1996, 1997 and 1998 E. C., respectively. According to BoFED (April 2004), at least 1.8 quintals of cereal production (e.g. wheat) on average per head per year is essential for food self-sufficiency. S0, one can conclude that food self-sufficiency has been achieved in recent years in the study wereda. However, there are constraints, including absence of a stable extension approach, shortage of trained personnel in the field and unstable personnel structure in the sector at each level. Besides, there is an apparent hesitation among farmers to adopt modern technology, including fertilizer utilization, due to previous failures. Farmers sensitized by development agents to use fertilizer may not get the expected yield due to natural adversities which result in the development of negative attitudes among some farmers through time.

In addition to this, although the government's ambition is to bring about radical change in water resource exploitation capacity, the performance of adopting running water-harvesting technologies such as pond construction is not producing the desired results in Legambo Wereda due to different reasons. Some of the problems include: poor technical support on the part of the government, and inability to afford construction costs on the part of farmers. However, the wereda registered good performance in small-scale irrigation development in recent years although it is minimal to achieve the food security goal, as the wereda is a drought-prone one in the Region. The size of irrigated land was less than five hundred hectares previously, but almost doubled in 1996 E.C. It is about three-fold and four-fold in the following consecutive years. On the other hand, there are formal directives introduced by local administrators that each farmer is expected to cover his/her plot of land with a terrace, following the wereda decentralization program. It is reported that there is good achievement in this respect. However, it may not be sustainable due to the limitation in terms of attitudinal change.

4. Conclusion

There is a commendable achievement in implementation of some aspects of ANRS' wereda decentralization program despite existing critical constraints. Among the achievements, the effort to make the three branches of government independent of each other at each level, the effort to decentralize power to wereda government structures, the effort to launch a pool system and the application of fiscal decentralization, and the effort to generate resources from the people for local development instead of waiting for government subsidy, are the main ones. Although there are obstacles in its implementation here and there, the Civil Service Reform that has been implemented in parallel has a positive impact on achievements. On the other hand, shortage of well-trained, experienced and committed pool of humanpower is one of the main challenges of decentralization program in ANRS. The second main challenge is lack of competence among members of the political leadership. The source of such shortcomings is directly or indirectly associated not only with the supply of highly trained personnel in the country but also with the lack of intensive training and motivation for existing staff and political leaders. Besides, there is a gap to ensure dynamic structural and organizational setups. Therefore, the following are the main concerns to be addressed properly for the success of wereda decentralization program.

a) To achieve the desired level of ramification of wereda decentralization in terms of active involvement of the people, awareness creation related activities should be priority areas of the Regional as well as local governments. Training should also be an intensive one to bring about significant impact in terms of building competence among trainees. Furthermore, the capacity building effort in the Region should focus on self-sufficiency of wereda and zonal structures in order to build self-confidence among local governments for self-development.

b) To improve transparency and accountability in each hierarchy of government, constitutional provisions should be translated into practices as intended. wereda councils and executives (cabinet) should stand independent of each other in all aspects, including financial and personnel administration. Besides, there should be continuous oversight scheme by using the full time of established committees. At least, the speakers, deputy speakers and chairpersons of the established committees should work in a continuous manner throughout the year.

c) In the context of ANRS, characterized by poor infrastructure and information-communication services especially in the rural areas, governmental hierarchies should be structured by taking this fact in to consideration. One of the alternatives to fill the gap in this respect could be strengthening zonal structures legally and fiscally, and zones should be able to command the services of qualified personnel. The business process reengineering practices already underway in this respect should be strengthened. Special attention should be given to ensuring the deployment of qualified personnel in the whole decentralization program implementation. Alternative solutions in this respect should be aimed at not only retaining existing civil servants in their organization, but also creating a fertile ground to attract well trained, experienced and committed personnel in rural weredas. Attention should also be given to basic office infrastructures such as computer, fax and Internet services. The Wereda-net program may have a positive impact in this respect if it is made fully operational as fast as possible.

d) As fiscal decentralization is the major aspect of wereda decentralization program, its application should be facilitated by addressing gaps in terms of ensuring local governments meaningful participation and in terms of ensuring credible data flow for decision on the block grant fiscal transfer. Ensuring credible audit system in intra-wereda budget utilization should also be the immediate task of the Regional Government in order to safeguard the decentralization program. In addition, there should be the consent of the people in local fund raising and related issues from the beginning of plan implementation. Here, it is important to make use of the informal structures and networks to ensure active involvement of the people at grassroots level. Community indigenous institutions such as "idir" should be considered as grassroots level development promotion and implementation centers. Great emphasis should be given to quality in delivery of basic services such as education and health in parallel with service coverage expansion. As the Civil Service Reform is the backbone for achieving decentralization program objectives, its implementation should use self-initiating and motivating mechanisms among the civil servants themselves as much as possible. Besides, the evaluation forum (the so-called "gimgema") should be implemented by avoiding subjectivity as much as possible. It should also be a constructive one rather than using for fault-finding and penalizing purposes.

Bibliography

Amhara National Regional State (ANRS). 2004. Development indicators of Amhara National Regional State. Bahir Dar.

_____. August 2003. Public Sector Capacity Building Action Plan (PSCAP) 2003/4-2007-2007/8. Final Draft. Bahir Dar (unpublished). Bahir Dar.

_____. 2001. The Revised Constitution of the Amhara National Regional State Approved Proclamation. Zikre Hig Gazete, Proclamation No.59/2001, November 5th. Bahir Dar.

_____. April 1997. Wereda's Block Grant Subsidy Formula. Finance and Economic Development Bureau. Bahir Dar. (Amharic version, unpublished). Bahir Dar.

_____. 1995. The Proclamation of the Constitution of the Amhara National Region. Bahir Dar. Zikre Hig Gazete, Proclamation No-2/1995, June, 22nd. Bahir Dar.

_____. Government Structural Taskforce (1994 E.C.) Wereda Organizational Structure Final Document. Bahir Dar. (Amharic version, unpublished). Bahir Dar.

Anton, J. Thomas. 1989. *American federalism and public policy: How the system works*. New York: Random House.

Barkan, Joil, *et al*. 1998. Democratization in Sub-Saharan Africa. Occasional Papers 45 through 49. International Programs, University of Iowa.

Bahru Zewde and Siegfrid Pausewany. 2002. *Ethiopia: The challenge of democracy from below*. Uppsala: Nordiska Afrikainstitute; Addis Ababa: Forum for Social Studies.

Bureau of Finance and Economic Development (BOFED). April 2004. Annual Statistical Bulletin, 2003/2004. Bahir Dar.

Boro, H. Sylvaun. 2002. *Decentralization and reform in Africa*. Boston, London: Kluwer.

Buthelezi, Sipho, and Abdalla Bujra. 2000. *Leadership, civil society and decentralization in Africa: Case studies from Southern Africa*. Addis Ababa: Development Policy Management Forum (DPFM).

Distance Learning and Research Center Seminar Series on Governance (S8). 2004. Improving good governance through strengthening the local governance. Rome, Addis Ababa, New Delhi, Abuja, April27-28 and May 3-4.

El-Battahani, Atta. 2000. Crises, politics and governance in Sudan. Regional Conference on Promoting Good Governance and Wider Civil Society Participation in Eastern and Southern Africa. 6-8 November, Addis Ababa.

Eshetu Cholle, ed. 1994. Fiscal decentralization in Ethiopia. Addis Ababa.

Fenta Mandefro. 1998. Decentralization in post-Derg Ethiopia. Aspects of Federal-Regional relation. Masters Thesis, Addis Ababa University.

FDRE. 1995. The Constitution of the Federal Democratic Republic of Ethiopia. Federal Negarit Gazeta, Proclamation No.1/1995. Addis Ababa.

Gonneratne, Wilbert, and R.A. Obduho, eds. 1997. *Contemporary issues in regional development policy: Perspective in Eastern and Southern Africa*. USA: Ashgate.

Hailu Belay. 2003. The current decentralization process in Ethiopia: Prospects and challenges. Working Paper, No. 14, RLDS, Addis Ababa University.

Helmising, A.H.J. Bert. 2002. Decentralization and empowerment: Issues in the local government debate. Inaugural Address as Professor of Local and Regional Planning, at the University of UTREHT.

House of Federation. February 2002. Federalism and decentralization. Ethio-German Cooperation. Unpublished.

Ibrahim Edris. (n.d.). Promotion of the culture of democracy and good governance at the federal and regional level: Strategies for the implementation of human rights and freedoms enshrined in the FDRE Constitution. Addis Ababa.

International Monetary Fund (IMF). February 2004. The FDRE: Poverty Reduction Strategy Paper Annual Progress Report. Washington, D.C. IMF.
_____. 2005. The Federal Democratic Republic of Ethiopia: Selected Issues and Statistical Appendix. IMF country report No. 05/28.

Kassahun Berhanu. 2000. Decentralization and governance: The Ethiopian experience. Regional Conference on Promoting Good Governance and Wider Civil Society Participation in Eastern and Southern Africa. 6-8 November. Addis Ababa.

Legambo Wereda Public Participation and Organization Affaires Office. 1997 E.C.. Office Document. Legambo, Akesta (unpublished).

Legambo Wereda Administrative Council Office. 1996 and 1997 E.C.   Office Document. Legambo, Akesta (unpublished).

Legambo Wereda Finance and Planning, Education, Agriculture and Rural Development Offices. 1997 and 1998 E.C. Statistical Data. Legambo, Akesta. (Unpublished).

Loop, Theo van der, ed. 2002. Local democracy and decentralization in Ethiopia: RLDS/AAU, Addis Ababa, and UN-HABITAT, Nairobi.

Mehret Ayenew. 1998. Some preliminary observations on institutional and administrative gaps in Ethiopia's decentralization process. Working Paper, No.1. RLDS, Addis Ababa University

Ministry of Capacity Building (MoCB). October 2004. District Level Decentralization Program (DLDP) Action Plan (2005- 2008). Federal DLDP public sector Capacity Building Program document, Addis Ababa. Unpublished.

Ministry of Finance and Economic Development (MOFED) July 2002. Ethiopia: Sustainable Development and Poverty Reduction Program. Addis Ababa.

Mwanje, Justus Inonda. 2001. *Qualitative research process*. Addis Ababa: Organization for Social Science Research in Eastern and Southern Africa (OSSREA).

Nahu Asteraye. 2004. Fiscal decentralization. Ethiopian Civil Service College. Addis Ababa. Unpublished

Pratchett, Lwrence, and David Willion, eds. 1996. *Local democracy and local government*. UK: Macmillan.

Selolwane, Doo Onalenna. 2000. The challenge of consolidating good governance and politics. Regional Conference on Promoting Good Governance and Wider Civil Society Participation in Eastern and Southern Africa. 6-8 November 2000. Addis Ababa.

Tegegn Gebre-Egziabher. 2001. The institutional environment of local planning in Ethiopia with an example from Amhara Region. Research Fellow Series, Institute of Economics, Japan.

Treisman, Daniel. December 2003. Decentralization and the quality of government. Department of Political Science, University of California, Los Angeles.

UN-Habitat. 2002. Local democracy and decentralization in East and Southern Africa. A publication of Global Campaign on Urban Governance.

Vaughan, Sarah, and Kietil Tronvoll. 2003. The culture of power in contemporary Ethiopia's political life. Sida Studies, Edita Severg AB.

Vaillancourt, Fransous, and Richard Bird. 1998. *Fiscal decentralization in developing countries*. Cambridge University Press.

Worku Yehuwalashet. 2004. District level decentralization in Ethiopia: Expenditure assignment and fiscal transfer. DLDP, Ministry of Capacity Building. Unpublished.

World Bank. 1992. *Poland's decentralization and reform of the State*. Washington, D.C.: World Bank.

_____. Feb. 2002. Ethiopia: The wereda studies. World Bank country office in Ethiopia. Addis Ababa.

www.ingramcontent.com/pod-product-compliance
Lightning Source LLC
Chambersburg PA
CBHW021828020426
42334CB00014B/535